DOCUMENTING HISTORY

WORLD WAR I
1914–18

CHRISTINE HATT

FRANKLIN WATTS
A Division of Scholastic Inc.

NEW YORK TORONTO LONDON AUCKLAND SYDNEY
MEXICO CITY NEW DELHI HONG KONG
DANBURY, CONNECTICUT

First published by Evans Brothers Limited, 2000
2A Portman Mansions
Chiltern Street
London
W1M ILE

First American edition 2001 by Franklin Watts
A Division of Scholastic Inc.
90 Sherman Turnpike
Danbury, CT 06816

Catalog details are available from the Library of Congress
Cataloging-in-Publication Data

Printed in Spain by GRAFO

Design – Neil Sayer
Editorial – Nicola Barber
Maps – Tim Smith
Consultant – Nigel Steel, Head of the Research and
 Information Office, Imperial War Museum, London
Production – Jenny Mulvanny

Title page picture: *Over the Top* by British painter
 Paul Nash (see page 34)

Border: A World War I tank

ISBN 0-531-14611-1 (Lib. Bdg.)

ACKNOWLEDGMENTS

For permission to reproduce copyright pictorial material, the author and publishers gratefully acknowledge the following:

Cover (background image, centre and bottom left) Topham Picturepoint (top left, top right and bottom right) Mary Evans Picture Library
title page Topham Picturepoint **page 7** (top) Mary Evans Picture Library (bottom) Popperfoto **page 8** Popperfoto **page 9** Mary Evans Picture Library **page 10** Topham Picturepoint **page 11** (top and bottom) Mary Evans Picture Library **page 12** Popperfoto **page 13** Mary Evans Picture Library **page 15** (top) e.t. archive (bottom) Kensington Library Special Collection **page 17** (top and bottom) e.t. archive **page 18** Topham Picturepoint **page 20** Popperfoto **page 21** (top) Popperfoto (bottom) Topham Picturepoint **page 22** e.t. archive **page 23** e.t. archive **page 24** (top right) Topham Picturepoint (bottom left) Popperfoto **page 25** (top and bottom) Mary Evans Picture Library **page 26** Hulton Getty **page 27** (right) Mary Evans Picture Library (bottom left) Topham Picturepoint **page 28** (top) Topham Picturepoint (bottom) Popperfoto **page 29** (middle and bottom) Mary Evans Picture Library **page 30** (top left) Mary Evans Picture Library (bottom right) Popperfoto **page 31** (top) Popperfoto (bottom) Topham Picturepoint **page 33** Topham Picturepoint **page 34** (top right) Topham Picturepoint (bottom left) Popperfoto **page 35** e.t. archive **page 36** (left) Popperfoto (right) Topham Picturepoint **page 37** (left) Hulton Getty (bottom right) Topham Picturepoint **page 38** (top) Topham Picturepoint (bottom) The Kobal Collection **page 39** (left) From the papers of D J Sweeney, at the Department of Documents in The Imperial War Museum (right) Popperfoto **page 40** (left) Topham Picturepoint (right) Mary Evans Picture Library **page 41** Topham Picturepoint **page 42** (top) Popperfoto (bottom) Topham Picturepoint **page 43** (top) e.t. archive (bottom) Mary Evans Picture Library **page 44** Hulton Getty **page 45** Mary Evans Picture Library **page 46** Popperfoto **page 47** (top) Popperfoto (bottom) e.t. archive **page 48** Popperfoto **page 49** (top) e.t archive (bottom) Topham Picturepoint **page 51** Topham Picturepoint **page 52** (top right) e.t. archive (bottom) Topham Picturepoint **page 53** e.t. archive (bottom) With thanks to the Kensington Library Special Collections **page 54** (top) Hulton Getty (bottom) Mary Evans Picture Library **page 56** e.t. archive **page 57** (top and bottom) Hulton Getty **page 58** Popperfoto **page 59** Popperfoto

For permission to reproduce copyright material for the documents, the author and publisher gratefully acknowledge the following:

page 9, **page 11** (top), **page 39** (bottom), **page 57** (bottom) From *Historic Documents of World War 1* by Louis L. Snyder. Published by Greenwood Press, Connecticut **page 11** (bottom), **page 31** *The Virago Book of Women and The Great War 1914-1918*, published by Little, Brown and Co, London **page 13** (middle), **page 21** (bottom), **page 33**, **page 55** (bottom) *A French Soldier's War Diary 1914-1918*. Published by The Elmfield Press, Yorkshire, 1975 **page 13** (bottom), **page 15**, **page 29** (bottom) From *An English Wife in Berlin*, courtesy of Kensington Library **page 17** (middle), **page 43**, **page 37** (bottom), **page 51** From *The Imperial War Museum Book of the Western Front* by Malcolm Brown (London: Sidgwick & Jackson, 1993), with thanks to the Imperial War Museum Department of Documents and to the copyright holders of each document **page 17** (bottom), **page 35** (top) From *Voices & Images of the Great War* by Lyn Macdonald, reproduced by permission of Penguin UK **page 19** (top), **page 21** (middle) *With a Machine Gun to Cambrai* by George Coppard **page 19** (bottom), **page 29** (middle) *Goodbye To All That* by Robert Graves, Carcanet Press Limited **page 23** From *The Great War and the Shaping of the 20th Century*, published by Penguin Puttnam Inc. **page 27** (middle) *From U-Boat to Concentration Camp*, published by William Hodge and Co., Glasgow **page 35** (bottom) *The Farmer Remembers the Son*, from 'The Camp', Sidney J. Endacott, 1920 **page 37** From *The Red Baron*, published by Bailey Brothers & Swinfen Limited, Folkestone **page 53** *All Quiet on the Western Front* by Erich Maria Remarque. "m Westen Nichts Neues," copyright 1928 by Ullstein A. G.; Copyright renewed © 1956 by Erich Maria Remarque. "All Quiet on the Western Front," copyright 1929, 1930 by Little, Brown and Company; Copyright renewed © 1957, 1958 by Erich Maria Remarque. All rights reserved. **page 55** (middle) The extract from *Testament of Youth* by Vera Brittain is reproduced by permission of Mark Bostridge and Rebecca Williams, her literary executors. **page 58** (middle) By permission of The Society of Authors, on behalf of the Laurence Binyon Estate

Every effort has been made to trace copyright holders but in some cases this has not proved possible. The publisher will be happy to rectify any such errors or omissions in future reprints and/or new editions.

CONTENTS

LOOKING AT DOCUMENTS

The war that broke out in Europe during the summer of 1914 and lasted until late 1918 was different from any previous conflict. It was different in scale because a struggle that at first had just five main participants—Britain, France, Russia, Germany, and Austria-Hungary—eventually involved soldiers from five continents, making it the first *world* war. It was also different in nature because of the new weapons, vehicles, and tactics used, and because civilian populations were affected as never before.

World War I tells the story of more than four years of terrible strife. It explores the political situation that set the scene for war, as well as its immediate causes. It traces the course of the fighting, from the early "war of movement," through the grim years of trench warfare, to the final offensives. It looks closely at the wartime experiences of many people, from great military leaders to working women on the home fronts. Finally, it briefly examines the political and social changes that swept the world after the armistice was signed.

To bring this story to life, *World War I* draws on a wide range of documents, including official treaties, letters written by soldiers, propaganda leaflets, diaries, and newspaper reports. You will also find excerpts from some of the many novels and poems inspired by the war, written both during and after the war. To make the documents easy to read, we have printed them in modern type. Difficult or old-fashioned words or phrases are explained in labels around the text. Photographs of the original documents appear alongside some excerpts.

When you are looking at a document, think carefully about its origin. Was it written at the start of the war, when no one realized how bloody the fighting would be, or later, when the conflict had claimed thousands of lives? Who wrote it—a politician who had never been to the front or a soldier who had experienced the horrors of battle? Is it propaganda, more concerned with boosting morale than telling the truth? These and similar questions will help you figure out how reliable a document is likely to be. But remember that no single document can give you a full picture of an event as complex and momentous as World War I.

On these two pages are a few excerpts from the documents used in this book. They have been selected to give you an idea of the variety of documents included, and to explain how and why some were written.

Many great works of imaginative literature were written by soldiers who participated in the war, and you will find excerpts from several of them in this book. This verse comes from a poem by Vance Palmer, an Australian soldier who fought in the terrible Battle of the Somme (see page 35).

I have returned to these;
The farm, and kindly Bush, and the young calves lowing;
But all that my mind sees
Is a quaking bog in a mist—stark, snapped trees,
And **the dark Somme flowing.**

What does this mean? Some words or phrases are difficult to understand. The captions alongside the documents give explanations of highlighted areas of text. You can find out where the **Somme** was on page 35.

Diaries written by people who lived through the war provide invaluable information about day-to-day activities, either on the fighting fronts or among civilians far from the battle zones. *A French Soldier's War Diary 1914–18* gives an insight into the everyday life of a soldier (see pages 13 and 21).

We are living in the earth, our clothes are thick with dirt, we are itching all over, in our shoes, in our trousers, under our shirts, we can't even nod off for one single moment. Even if the guns are silent, the bugs keep on crawling...

Newspaper reports, interviews, and advertisements help to build up a picture of wartime life, as well as highlight particular events that took place during the war years. In 1915, the German government placed this advertisement (see page 27) in the American newspaper *New York World*. Most passengers who were about to sail on the *Lusitania* took little notice and the ship was sunk with hundreds on board.

The sinking of the *Lusitania*

Travellers intending to embark on the Atlantic voyage are reminded that a state of war exists between Germany and her allies; that the zone of war includes the waters adjacent to the British Isles; that, in accordance with formal notice given by the Imperial German Government, vessels flying the flag of Great Britain, or of any of her allies, are liable to destruction in those waters ...

Government documents from the war years provide an official view of the conflict. In his memoirs, British general Douglas Haig (left), quotes the telegram sent to him by the government after the terrible Battle of Passchendaele in 1917 (see page 45).

The War Cabinet desire to congratulate you and the troops under your command upon the achievements of the British Armies in Flanders in the great battle which has been raging since July 31st...

ORIGINS
EMPIRES AND ALLIANCES

The German ruler, Kaiser Wilhelm II (above left), and the British king, George V, were cousins. The family resemblance is clear in this photograph, which dates from 1913.

In the late nineteenth- and early twentieth-century, the most powerful nations in Europe formed two opposing alliances. Conflict between them grew, creating conditions for war long before troops went into action in 1914.

The German Empire was formed in 1871, following victory in war against France (see page 9). Kaiser Wilhelm II, ruler of Germany from 1888, was determined to turn his empire into a world power, so he built up its industry and its armed forces. In particular, the Kaiser set out to create a navy that would rival Britain's fleet. As a result of this arms race, tension between the two nations grew rapidly.

In 1882, Germany had joined Austria-Hungary and Italy to form the Triple Alliance. These three

allies, known as the Central Powers, agreed to help each other in the event of enemy attack. Germany was the alliance's most powerful member. Italy had become a united kingdom in 1861 but was weak and anxious to avoid a war. The Austro-Hungarian Empire was crumbling and its emperor, Franz Josef, struggled to control its eleven nations. Franz Josef also feared Serbia, which aimed to take over some imperial territory (see page 10).

Early twentieth-century Britain, ruled by George V from 1910, was a powerful industrial nation with a worldwide empire. The country's main protector was its mighty navy, so its army was relatively small and military service was not compulsory (as it was in

EUROPEAN ALLIANCES

Triple Entente	
Triple Alliance (Central Powers)	

0   310 miles
0   500 km

Factories owned by the Krupp family played a major role in Germany's industrialization program. They produced steel for shipbuilding, as well as the heavy artillery used to bombard enemy lines during World War I.

other major European countries). Britain was eager to preserve its own position of power in northern Europe, so it viewed Germany's military buildup with suspicion.

After its defeat in the Franco-Prussian War (1870–71), France lost the provinces of Alsace and Lorraine to Germany. This was a great blow to French national pride and the government vowed to win them back. Anti-German feeling in France made the country a natural ally for Britain. So, in 1904, the two nations formed the Entente Cordiale.

The Russian Empire was ruled by Czar Nicholas II from 1894. Its army was huge but poorly equipped. Russians had no desire for war, but were ready to support the Serbs, their fellow Slavs, against Austria-Hungary. In 1907, the Russians allied with Britain and France to form the Triple Entente. This meant that the Triple Alliance faced potential enemies to the east and west. War seemed likely—Germany believed it was inevitable.

BELGIAN NEUTRALITY

In 1839, all the major European powers, including Prussia (later part of the German Empire), signed the Treaty of London. It declared that Belgium should remain permanently neutral in any future conflict. Germany's failure to abide by this agreement played an important role in the eventual outbreak of war (see page 10).

On October 28, 1908, an interview with Kaiser Wilhelm II appeared in the British *Daily Telegraph* newspaper. In it, he assured readers that he had no desire for war. Unfortunately, his forceful language gave the opposite impression.

Here the Kaiser gives his reasons for the growth of the German navy (see pages 26–27).

Assign any bounds means "put any limits."

Manifold means "many different."

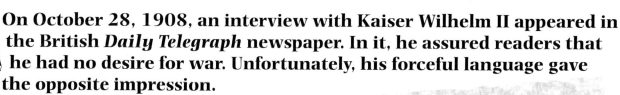

But, you will say, what of the German navy? Surely, that is a menace to England?... My answer is clear. Germany is a young and growing empire. She has a world-wide commerce which is rapidly expanding, and to which the legitimate ambition of patriotic Germans refuses to **assign any bounds**. Germany must have a powerful fleet to protect that commerce and her **manifold** interests in even the most distant seas. She expects those interests to go on growing, and she must be able to champion them manfully in any quarter of the globe. Her horizons stretch far away...

THE ROAD TO WAR

On June 28, 1914, Archduke Franz Ferdinand, heir to the Austro-Hungarian throne, made an official visit to the city of Sarajevo in Bosnia-Herzegovina. His beloved wife Sophie accompanied him. The events that took place on that day finally plunged the world into war.

Bosnia-Herzegovina had been an official part of the Austro-Hungarian Empire since 1908. Its people were Slavs, many of them Serbs. They believed strongly that their nation should be part of the neighboring Slav state of Serbia. The Serbians shared this view. Some people were prepared to use violence to gain independence from the Austro-Hungarian Empire—including members of a secret society known as the Black Hand.

As Archduke Franz Ferdinand set off through Sarajevo in an open-topped car, seven members of the Black Hand were lying in wait for him. They planned to assassinate the Archduke as part of their campaign for independence. Six of the men failed, but the seventh, nineteen-year-old Gavrilo Princip, shot and killed both Franz Ferdinand and his wife. Their deaths brought political crisis to Europe.

Austria-Hungary decided to take a strong stand against Serbia, which it believed had supported this act of terrorism. But first Emperor Franz Josef consulted Kaiser Wilhelm II. He wanted to be sure that, if war did break out in the Balkans, Germany would come to Austria-Hungary's aid. The emperor got the assurances he wanted, then took the next step towards conflict. On July 23, he sent Serbia an ultimatum.

The ultimatum required Serbia to root out all organizations that were plotting against Austria-Hungary. When Serbia replied on July 25, it agreed to this demand. Austria-Hungary, however, had already decided war was necessary. War was declared at 11:10 AM on July 28, 1914.

At once, the system of alliances began to operate. Germany had already agreed to back Austria-Hungary, its partner in the Triple Alliance, but Italy remained neutral. Russia sided with the Serbs. France backed Russia, its partner in the Triple Entente. Then, on August 3, Germany invaded neutral Belgium in order to reach France. This prompted Britain to join its French and Russian allies the next day. The United States remained neutral at first, as Congress feared that the warring European countries would appeal to the various—and large—immigrant groups at home.

When they set off for France in August 1914, German soldiers expected an easy victory and a speedy return home. One of the chalked messages on this train car indicates their optimistic mood. It says "Ausflug nach Paris"— "Excursion to Paris."

Like Gavrilo Princip, Borijove Jevtic set out to murder Archduke Franz Ferdinand on June 28, 1914. This extract is taken from his account of that day's events which appeared in the *New York World* newspaper on June 29, 1924.

An artist's impression of the double assassination in Sarajevo

...we knew what we would do to Francis [Franz] Ferdinand. We would kill him to show Austria there yet lived within its borders defiance of its rule. We would kill him to bring once more to the boiling point the fighting spirit of the revolutionaries and pave the way for revolt... As the car came abreast [Princip] stepped forward from the curb, drew his automatic pistol from his coat and fired two shots. The first struck the wife of the Archduke... in the **abdomen**... The second struck the Archduke close to the heart. He uttered only one word, "Sofia" – a call to his stricken wife. Then his head fell back and he collapsed.

Abdomen is another word for "stomach."

Herbert Henry Asquith was the British Prime Minister in 1914. He was present in the Houses of Parliament on August 4 when Britain's decision to enter the war was announced. IIis wife, Margot, recalled what happened next in her autobiography.

The **Speaker** is the official who keeps order in the House of Commons, the elected chamber of the Houses of Parliament.

The declaration was made in the name of King George V.

When the **Speaker** had finished reading the **King's message** all the members poured out of the House, and I went down to the Prime Minister's room... I sat down beside him with a feeling of numbness in my limbs... Henry [the Prime Minister] sat at his writing-table leaning back with a pen in his hand... I got up and leant my head against his: we could not speak for tears. When I arrived in **Downing Street** I went to bed. How did it—how could it have happened?... [later] the clock on the mantelpiece hammered out the hour, and when the last beat of midnight struck it was silent as dawn. We were at War.

10 Downing Street is the London home of the Prime Minister.

Margot Asquith

Chapter 2

1914

The Schlieffen Plan

The German Invasion of France

The Germans wanted to win the war quickly and decisively. In order to do so, they believed that it was essential to avoid fighting France and Russia at the same time. In 1905, Count Alfred von Schlieffen, then Chief of the General Staff, had drawn up a plan to avoid this problem.

The aim of the Schlieffen Plan was to take Paris, defeat the French, and only then deal with the Russian threat in the east. However, in 1914 events did not unfold as the Kaiser and Helmut von Moltke, now Chief of the General Staff, had hoped. The Germans set out for France via Belgium, crossing the border on August 4. The badly equipped Belgian army resisted with unexpected vigor. Nevertheless, the Germans crossed the country in about three weeks. Thousands of refugees fled ahead of them.

The French, led by General Joseph Joffre, were better-prepared than the Germans had believed. Their "Plan XVII" swung into action as soon as war broke out. Its main aim was to attack the Germans in Alsace and Lorraine (see page 9), then push on to Germany's capital, Berlin. Some troops were also to resist the German invasion of Belgium.

Plan XVII was a failure. French swords and guns were no match for the German heavy artillery in Alsace-Lorraine—more than 40,000 Frenchmen died there between August 20 and 23. The survivors retreated into France, where they joined the armies trying to push back the Germans. But the French were still overcome easily.

Germany had hoped Great Britain would stay out of the fighting. But the British Expeditionary Force (BEF), led by Sir John French, set out for Belgium soon after it was invaded. On August 23, the BEF met a large German army at Mons. Following a day-long battle, the British were forced to retreat south into France.

The French had been pushed back to the Marne River, where the retreating British joined them. The Germans were just 24.8 miles from Paris. But instead of heading west and attacking the city as planned, the exhausted German troops turned east to the Marne. Meanwhile, Joffre brought French reinforcements from Paris. At the Battle of the Marne which took place from September 5 to 9, France and Britain forced Germany back to the Aisne River. In the west, the Schlieffen Plan was shattered.

General Helmut von Moltke

A line of Belgian refugees lining up for food handouts

Henri Desagneaux served in the French army during World War I. Many years later, in 1971, his diary of the war was published. This excerpt from *Journal de Guerre 14–18* (*A French Soldier's War Diary, 1914–18*) tells of the refugees who made their way across France during the early days of the fighting in 1914.

Nags is an informal word for "horses."

The **bourgeois** means "the middle class."

Requisition officers were military officials responsible for collecting goods and equipment that the armed forces needed in wartime.

25 August, Tuesday
Refugees arrive from all directions, a mixture of every class of society: the peasant carrying his little bundle; the worker with a few old clothes; small farmers, shopkeepers with their cases, finally the bourgeois, dragging along a dog or a trunk... Men, women, children, and old folk are huddled together in any vehicles they could find. What a sad sight it is to see the old carts drawn by nags that even the requisition officers refused; these poor people, distressed, leaving their homes and their possessions, without knowing whether they will return.

Evelyn, Princess Blücher, was a British woman who was married to a German count. She spent 1914–18 in Berlin, and in 1921 published a memoir of those years. Here she describes how hard it was for both the German and the British public to find out what was really happening.

This was untrue propaganda.

BERLIN, September 18, 1914.– Strange that we hear so little of the fighting round Paris. We have all been expecting to hear of their [the Germans'] triumphant entry every day. The fighting, they say, is very hard, and there are tremendous losses on either side, but I am beginning to think the tide has turned against the Germans, hence this sudden silence... We have at last discovered means of buying the Times [newspaper]... at last we can see what the English are really doing or thinking... What curious reports are being circulated... Berlin is in flames, and in a state of starvation, panic, and revolution. How shall we ever know the truth in any country?

THE EASTERN FRONT

The ill-fated Schlieffen Plan underestimated the Russians, as well as the British and French. The Germans had assumed the vast Russian army would take at least six weeks to get into action in the east. But they were wrong, and their miscalculation cost them severely.

Russia had about 1.5 million permanent soldiers. On August 7, about 370,000 of them, in two separate armies, invaded Germany. Meanwhile, three million more Russians were mobilized. The swift Russian invasion realized the Germans' worst fear—they would have to fight on two fronts, the Eastern and the Western, at the same time. General von Moltke immediately sent more troops

east, weakening his forces in Belgium. He also placed two new commanders at the head of the Eastern Front armies, Paul von Hindenburg and Erich Ludendorff.

The Russian forces easily outnumbered the Germans. However, they were badly trained, led, and equipped—there was just one machine-gun for every thousand men. Many soldiers did not even have their own rifle. The commanders of the two armies, Alexander Samsonov and Pavel Rennenkampf, hated each other, so they did not communicate well. Finally, the Russians' radio messages were not coded, so the Germans quickly discovered their battle plan.

The plan was straightforward. The two Russian armies would separate to make their way around the Masurian Lakes in Germany's northeast corner. Then they would come together again, trapping the unsuspecting German troops between them. However, once the Germans became aware of what was intended, one of their leaders, Lieutenant Colonel Max Hoffmann, devised a counter-plan. The German forces would strike while the Russian armies were still apart.

Samsonov's army was the first to arrive west of the lakes. From August 26 to 31, it was overwhelmingly defeated by the Germans at the Battle of Tannenberg. About eighty thousand Russians were killed—almost all

THE EASTERN FRONT 1914–16

German troops advance into a village during the Battle of Tannenberg. Artillery fire has destroyed several of the buildings along the street.

the rest were taken prisoner. The Germans then headed east to attack Rennenkampf's army at the Masurian Lakes. About 125,000 Russian soldiers were killed during the second week of September. The remainder fled back to Russia. These were stunning German victories, but they were gained at the cost of diverting much-needed troops from the Western Front.

Evelyn, Princess Blücher

AUSTRO-HUNGARIAN ATTACKS

Austro-Hungarian armies were active in 1914, too. On the Eastern Front, they attacked the Russians in Galicia, far south of the German forces. Their early victories were reversed on September 8–12, when Russian troops led by Alexei Brusilov overcame them at Lemberg (see map page 14). The Austro-Hungarians invaded Serbia on August 12. They occupied the capital, Belgrade, on September 2, but were driven out by mid-December. About 200,000 Austro-Hungarian troops died in the fighting.

Posterity means "future generations."

In this second excerpt from her memoir, Evelyn, Princess Blücher (see page 13) describes the aftermath of Tannenberg, as reported in Germany.

BERLIN, October 14, 1914.—The victory of Tannenberg will go down to posterity as one of the most marvellous of modern times. Some of the horrors of it are so ghastly that an eye-witness, an officer, who has just returned from there, says it will live in his dreams to his dying day. The sight of thousands of Russians driven into two huge lakes or swamps to drown was ghastly, and the shrieks and cries of the dying men and horses he will never forget...

AN ENGLISH WIFE
IN BERLIN

A PRIVATE MEMOIR OF EVENTS, POLITICS, AND
DAILY LIFE IN GERMANY THROUGHOUT THE
WAR AND THE SOCIAL REVOLUTION OF 1918

BY

EVELYN, PRINCESS BLÜCHER

NINTH IMPRESSION

LONDON
CONSTABLE AND COMPANY Ltd.
1921

THE "RACE FOR THE SEA"

After the Battle of the Marne on the Western Front (see page 12), both Germany and the Allies (Britain and France) wanted to avoid another head-on clash. So they began the so-called "Race for the Sea."

This race was in part what its name suggests—a headlong dash northwest toward the English Channel. However, although both sides wanted to take control of the coastal ports, the main goal was to overtake the enemy by going around its flank (side). If successful, this would allow troops to wheel back and surround their opponents.

After the German retreat from the Marne, Helmut von Moltke was replaced by Erich von Falkenhayn. This strong general oversaw the German push toward

the sea, which was the first to begin. At the time, many German troops were still in Belgium, fighting for the town of Antwerp. When it fell on October 10, some moved west to join the forces heading for the coast.

French troops under Joffre and the British Expeditionary Force (BEF) under Sir John French quickly followed the Germans. Outflanking turned out to be impossible, but the opposing armies fought several battles. The most important took place at Ypres in Flanders. It began on October 12 and lasted for more than a month. The Germans rushed in about 100,000 extra, untrained men to try to seize a victory. But the Allies held the town.

This was no great triumph, however. Sir John French, leader

of the BEF, was weak and indecisive. About fifty thousand men in the BEF were killed or injured at Ypres. French casualties in the battle were also high—about 250,000 dead and wounded. The terrible losses on all sides came about not by victory but by stalemate.

Ypres marked a turning point. The early "war of movement" across large areas of ground ended there. It was replaced by an almost static "war of attrition," designed to wear down the enemy gradually. This new type of warfare was fought from trenches. The Germans had dug the first trenches by the Aisne River (see page 12). After Ypres, a 400-mile line of trenches was built, stretching from the coast almost to Switzerland.

THE WESTERN FRONT 1914–15

TRENCH TRUCES

When the war broke out, German troops were assured that the fighting would be over "before the leaves fall from the trees." The Allies expected victory to be theirs by Christmas. But by December, men on both sides were living in trenches. Many had learned to respect their enemies' bravery. On Christmas Eve 1914, German, French, and British soldiers sang carols, shouted greetings to enemy troops, or even met them in No Man's Land (see page 18). Officers soon put a stop to these truces.

By 1915, troops were once again prepared for combat.

British and German soldiers socializing in Belgium on Christmas Day, 1914

Lord Kitchener was the British Secretary of State for War from 1914. He realized that the country's professional army was not large enough, so he recruited hundreds of thousands of volunteers. In this letter, dated December 3, 1914, Captain E. Balfour, a BEF member, explains what he believes this will mean.

...the new Campaign is going to be fought and won by a great half-trained National Army—where you've got to take what you can get and not laugh at people for being a certain class or making fools of themselves. But if the old Army is going to be worth its salt and remain the backbone of the show, it's got without jealousy and in humbleness to allow itself to be absorbed into a less efficient whole ...

The man at the center of this British army recruitment poster is Lord Kitchener. His icy stare and pointing finger were hard to resist. The flags on the poster are those of the Allies in 1914 (from left to right: Belgium, Russia, the United Kingdom, France, and Japan).

Schnapps is a strong alcoholic drink popular in Germany.

In this excerpt, a German lieutenant named Johannes Niemann describes the events that took place during a truce at Christmas, 1914.

Next morning... my orderly threw himself into my **dugout** to say that both the Scottish and German soldiers had come out of the trenches... I grabbed my binoculars and... saw the incredible sight of our soldiers exchanging cigarettes, **schnapps** and chocolate with the enemy. Later... a real football match got underway.

A **dugout** was a shelter cut in a trench wall or floor.

TRENCH SYSTEMS

Western Front soldiers dug trenches to defend themselves against enemy fire. At first, these trenches were not much more than long, muddy holes. However, as the stalemate continued, complex trench systems developed.

Many early trenches were only head-height and had unsupported earth walls. The earth removed to create the trenches was piled up to form defensive banks, called parapets in front and *parados* behind. Gradually, both parapets and *parados* were reinforced with sandbags, and solid floors were built from duckboards. Wood was used to support trench sides. Some trenches were dug deeper, and coils of barbed wire were placed in front of them to deter enemy attacks.

Single trenches slowly grew into maze-like trench systems. Their layout varied according to the nationality of the army and the type of battlefield, but they shared many features (see diagram page 19). The trench area closest to the enemy was called the front line. From the foremost trench, the fire trench, men shot at their opponents. Fire trenches were built in a zigzag shape, so that if a shell exploded, its blast could not travel far. A cover trench was often built about 33 yards behind the fire trench. It held more troops, ready to defend the front line if the enemy broke through.

About 80 yards behind the front line were the support trenches, where more soldiers waited to be called into action. The British and Germans, but not usually the French, also had troops in reserve trenches even farther back. German trench systems grew ever more complex. Some eventually extended 14 miles from the front.

Running roughly at right angles between the defensive trenches were communications trenches. They were often filled with troops moving to and from the front, but they also provided a link with command posts, first-aid stations, and kitchens in the support and reserve trenches. Trench extensions called saps formed part of many trench systems, too. Some led partway to the enemy lines and were used as listening posts. There, soldiers tried to hear enemy activity through the mud walls.

The opposing front lines were separated by an area of open ground between about 76 yards and half a mile wide. This was "No Man's Land," where soldiers died in the hundreds of thousands.

British troops make their way along a trench in France. The sandbags and wooden wall supports can be seen clearly. The duckboards that form the floor are just visible beneath the men's feet.

OBSERVATION POSTS

Heavy guns, known as artillery, did not fire their shells from the trenches. They were based behind the lines and bombarded the enemy from there. However, artillerymen needed to know the exact positions of their targets to avoid wasting ammunition or even hitting their own lines. So they set up observation posts on the front line and relayed information back to their comrades using field telephones (see page 43).

George Coppard went to war when he was just sixteen years old. He was an ordinary private soldier who served as a machine gunner. In 1969, Coppard published *With a Machine Gun to Cambrai*, an account of his wartime experiences.

Six feet is about 1.8 m. One foot equals approximately 30 centimeters.

A **fire-step** was a small, raised platform at the front of a trench. By standing on the step, soldiers could see the enemy lines.

The trenches at le Touquet were in a very good condition, in parts almost like demonstration models. About **six feet** in depth from the top of the parapet, they were floored with duckboards, and were wide enough for two men to pass comfortably. A **fire-step** a foot or so high ran along each section of trench, enabling troops to adopt a good firing position in case of attack. The few dugouts that there were afforded very little more protection than a **shell-hole**. Most of them were just excavations at the bottom of a trench sufficient to crawl into and stretch out for sleep...

A **shell-hole** was a crater produced by a shell. Soldiers trapped in No Man's Land often hid in them.

Conditions in the support and reserve trenches were better than on the front line, especially for officers. In his autobiography *Goodbye to All That* (1929), the famous English poet and novelist Robert Graves tells of an officers' dugout in France.

This diagram shows a typical First World War trench system as seen from above.

At battalion headquarters, a dugout in the reserve line, about a quarter of a mile behind the front companies, the colonel... shook hands with us and offered us the whisky bottle... this dugout happened to be unusually comfortable, with an ornamental lamp, a clean cloth, and polished silver on the table... Pictures pasted on the papered walls; spring-mattressed beds, a gramophone, easy chairs: we found it hard to reconcile these with the accounts we had read of troops standing waist-deep in mud, and gnawing a biscuit while shells burst all around.

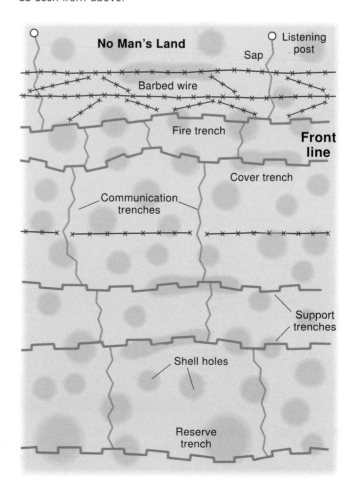

LIFE IN THE TRENCHES

The life of troops at the front veered between two extremes—day after day of boring routine followed by terrible outbreaks of fighting. The horrible living conditions, however, were a constant feature.

In theory, soldiers stayed in the front line for only about a week before a period of respite in the support or reserve trenches. However, replacements sometimes didn't arrive, forcing soldiers to remain at the front for two or even three times longer. After a tour of trench duty, men usually rested at billets behind the lines. There they organized plays, film shows, and sports events.

Days on the front line followed a routine. Attacks often began at dawn, so soldiers were awakened slightly earlier. They then prepared for possible enemy action, while sentries peered out over No Man's Land. After breakfast, men began their duties. Some repaired shell damage. Some collected mail, food, and ammunition from support and reserve trenches. Everyone cleaned their weapons and wrote letters home when they could. They also slept to make up for the hours spent working during the night. Sentries always kept watch, often using periscopes.

At night, soldiers ventured outside the trenches to carry out more dangerous jobs. Patrols repaired barbed wire defenses or gathered information at listening posts. Raiders made their way to enemy lines and launched ferocious surprise attacks. Men without special duties spent the night trying to sleep in damp, cramped dugouts.

Soldiers were always at risk from snipers (see document page 21), but the danger from the enemy was far greater during attacks. Before an attack began, artillery hurled shells into the trenches, causing serious injuries and deaths. Troops who went "over the top"—clambered out of the trenches to launch an attack—faced machine-gun fire and more shells. Troops whose trenches were captured faced grenades, rifles, bayonets, and knives. Inventions such as gas and tanks steadily added to this array of weapons.

Men developed strategies to cope with their grim lives. They formed close friendships, cracked jokes, sang, and sometimes grew very superstitious or religious. Many ordinary soldiers also developed a strong sense of comradeship with their enemy counterparts who were often seen as fellow-sufferers in a war devised by far distant officers and politicians.

A soldier looks through a periscope built into the wall of the trench. Periscopes were lifesavers because they allowed lookouts to watch enemy lines without turning themselves into sniper targets.

UNDERGROUND SQUALOR

The day-to-day squalor of life in the trenches was a constant challenge. Insufficient water for washing and unhygienic toilets spread disease. Rain turned the ground into mud and filthy water, and soldiers who stood in the mixture for too long developed trench foot. Rats infested the trenches. Not only did they steal men's food, they were also carriers of lice, whose bites caused illnesses such as trench fever. Lice clung to hair, skin and clothes, and soldiers spent hours removing them, a process that the British called "chatting."

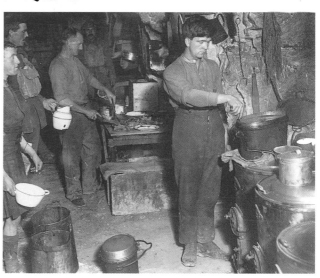

This underground kitchen on the Western Front trenches shows the dirty and unhygienic conditions in which troops were forced to live.

George Coppard (see page 19) explains how quickly snipers killed, and tells how a friend became a victim.

British troops called the Germans **Jerries**.

A **telescopic sighted rifle** is fitted with a mini-telescope that gives the user a good view of the target.

Stand to was the order given to British troops before dawn. Men had to take up their positions on the firesteps or in the trenches below.

Lulled by the quietness, someone would be foolish and carelessly linger with his head above the top of a parapet. Then, like a puppet whose strings have suddenly snapped, he crashes to the bottom of the trench... A **Jerry** sniper with a **telescopic sighted rifle**... has lain patiently, for hours perhaps, watching our parapet for the slightest movement... A pal of mine named Bill Bailey... died in this way... It was early morning and **stand to** was over. The fire was going nicely and the bacon was sizzling. I was sitting on the firestep and just as I was about to tuck in Bill crashed to the ground...

George Coppard in 1980

In this excerpt, Henri Desagneaux (see page 13) describes how the misery of being dirty and lice-infested added to the horror of battle.

When water was short, it could not be spared for shaving.

We are living in the earth, our clothes are thick with dirt, we are itching all over, in our shoes, in our trousers, under our shirts, we can't even nod off for one single moment. Even if the guns are silent, the bugs keep on crawling. God how filthy we are! **Fifteen days' growth of beard**, and for the last eighteen days I haven't taken my shoes off or had a change of underwear. We have no water to wash in, just mud all around us.

CHAPTER 3

1915

GALLIPOLI

THE GALLIPOLI CAMPAIGN

World War I entered a new phase in 1915. More countries joined the conflict, and the fighting spread beyond the Eastern and Western Fronts. The Allies' year began with an ill-fated attack on Turkey.

By the twentieth century, the six hundred-year-old Ottoman (Turkish) Empire was fading fast. However, the Central Powers welcomed it as an ally in October 1914. In 1915, British politician Winston Churchill suggested an attack on Turkey. He believed that the war would never be won in the trenches of Western Europe, but that Germany could be defeated by crushing its weaker ally. The Russians, whom the Turks had attacked on entering the war, were also calling for an Allied assault on Turkey.

Many politicians and military men opposed Churchill's plans. However, Lord Kitchener (see page 17) decided to go ahead. The aim of the campaign was to take over Constantinople, Turkey's capital. To do so, the British and French navies first set out to capture the Dardanelles—the strait of water that runs into the Sea of Marmara, on whose edge the city stands. Part of the battle plan was to destroy forts on the Gallipoli Peninsula, which forms the Dardanelles' northern coast.

The attack of the Peninsula began on February 19, 1915. Although it was partially successful, the Turkish gunners continued to fire, making it difficult for minesweepers to clear the seas of mines. Nevertheless, on March 18, the attacking navies tried to force their way through the Dardanelles. Mines blew up three ships and damaged three more. The officer in charge of the operation, Vice-Admiral John de Robeck, then called for assistance from land forces.

About 75,000 troops were sent to Gallipoli. In addition to British and French men, there were many Australians and New Zealanders (Anzacs). None had any battle experience. General Sir Ian Hamilton, who had only limited knowledge of Turkey and its army, was in command. The invasion began on April 25, with the main landings

General Sir Ian Hamilton (in the front on the far left) puts on a brave face as he leaves Gallipoli. Until 1915, he had been a successful military commander. After Gallipoli, he was never given a senior post again.

This painting shows the landing at Anzac Cove in April 1915. Turkish gunfire explodes all around the Allied soldiers as they scramble for cover. It has already hit one man, who lies wounded on the rocks.

THE SALONIKA FRONT

In September, 1915, Germany gained another ally—Bulgaria, a Balkan neighbor of Serbia. The Bulgarians hoped that if the Central Powers won the war, they would be granted a chunk of Serbian land. In October, British and French troops were sent to Salonika in northern Greece, which bordered Bulgaria and Serbia. They failed to prevent a Bulgarian invasion of Serbia, but thousands of Allied reinforcements were still sent to the region. There they remained for the rest of the war. They were known as the "forgotten army."

at Anzac Cove and Cape Helles. The Turks had strengthened their defenses and were able to resist most efforts to advance inland. The result was more fruitless trench warfare.

On August 6, a second wave of Allied invasions took place at Suvla Bay. They were also unsuccessful and the troops suffered in the sweltering summer heat. Finally, on December 7, the decision was made to evacuate. This process was completed by January 9, 1916. The whole disastrous campaign had cost about 46,000 Allied lives.

As members of the British Empire, Australia and New Zealand were soon drawn into the war. British incompetence and the courage of their own Anzac troops made Gallipoli a turning point. From then on, both countries felt they were to be truly independent nations. Keith Murdoch, an Australian journalist, expressed his personal views about Gallipoli in a letter to Australian Prime Minister Andrew Fisher. This is an excerpt from his letter.

Hamilton's poor planning and numerous other failures led to his dismissal in October 1915.

I visited most parts of Anzac [Cove] and Suvla Bay positions, walked many miles through the trenches, conversed with the leaders and what senior and junior officers I could reach, and was favored in all parts with full and frank confidence... This was always a hopeless scheme, after early May, and no one can understand why Hamilton persisted with it... A strong advance inland from Anzac has never been attempted. It is broken, rough, scrubby country, full of gullies and sharp ridges, and it is all within easy range of the Turkish forts at the Narrows... No serious advance could be made direct inland at this quarter.

THE EUROPEAN FRONTS

The war on the Western Front continued in 1915, but it lacked focus after the failure of the early plans. Cooperation between the French, under General Joseph Joffre, and the British, under Sir John French, was often reluctant and ineffective. On the Eastern Front, the Germans advanced far into Russian-controlled Poland.

On March 10, the British attacked the German line at Neuve Chapelle, France. The pre-battle attack was brief because of an ammunition shortage. As a result, the Germans had little warning and the British were able to take the village. However, a long wait for reinforcements and a collision between advancing troops gave the Germans time to strike back and the battle ended on March 12. This pattern of early success

Two British soldiers wearing primitive gas masks demonstrate how to use a Vermorel sprayer. It contained a chemical that neutralized chlorine, a gas that the Germans began to use as a weapon in 1915.

Sir John French

followed by collapse was to be repeated many times.

On April 22, the Germans launched an offensive at Ypres. During the battle, they used gas—chlorine—for the first time. It engulfed French troops, many of them from France's Algerian colony, as well as British and Canadian forces. The results were terrible but effective. However, the battle gave the

Germans no lasting advantage and ended on May 25.

The French launched a major offensive in the Champagne region on September 25. They broke through the German front line, but were unable to overcome strong second-line defenses and withdrew on October 6. Farther north, the British attacked and took Loos. But they again failed to build on their success because reinforcements were too far away. Sir John French continued the battle long after it was worthwhile, sacrificing thousands of lives. In December he was replaced by General Sir Douglas Haig.

Still disappointed by the defeat of Austria-Hungary in 1914 by the Russians at Lemberg, the Germans decided to support their ally in a counter-attack on Russian Poland in the east. On May 2, 1915, troops led by General August von Mackesen stormed into Galicia. Later, troops under Paul von Hindenburg advanced farther north. By November 1915, the Russians had retreated nearly 311 miles (500 km) and lost much of Poland. Russian ruler Czar Nicholas II and his people were completely humiliated—but determined to fight back.

THE ITALIAN FRONT

Like the Central Powers, the Allies gained new members in 1915. The most important was Italy. Before the war, Italy had been a partner of Germany and Austria-Hungary in the Triple

Alliance (see page 8). When war broke out, it remained neutral. Both sides then tried to gain Italy's allegiance by promising it a share of Austro-Hungarian land after the conflict was over. The Allies offered the bigger bribe, so, on May 23, 1915, Italy declared war on Austria-Hungary. Fighting on the Italian Front between the two countries was long and hard.

Italian troops fighting in the Alps in 1916

 This description of the aftermath of the 1915 Battle of Ypres comes from *A Fatalist at War* (1929), by German soldier Rudolf Binding.

Chlorine gas is greenish-yellow.

The effects of the successful gas attack were horrible. I am not pleased with the idea of poisoning men. Of course, the entire world will rage about it first and then imitate us. All the dead lie on their backs, with clenched fists; **the whole field is yellow**... The battlefield is fearful. One is overcome by a peculiar, sour, heavy, and penetrating smell of corpses. Rising over a plank bridge you find that its middle is supported only by the body of a long-dead horse. Men that were killed **last October** lie half in swamp and half in the yellow-sprouting beet-fields. The legs of an Englishman, still encased in **puttees**, stick out into a trench...

The first Battle of Ypres took place in October 1914.

Puttees formed part of the British army uniform. They were cloth strips wound around the lower half of the leg.

A German gas attack in 1915, photographed from the air

THE WAR AT SEA

Britain had ruled the seas for many years before World War I began, and the Royal Navy was the nation's pride. Kaiser Wilhelm II's determination to make the German High Seas Fleet equally strong was an important cause of the conflict.

The Kaiser, backed by Admiral Alfred von Tirpitz, started to build up his navy in the late nineteenth century. Soon afterward, Admiral Sir John Fisher, Britain's First Sea Lord, began to overhaul the Royal Navy and ordered a warship that would outperform all others. The result was the *Dreadnought*, launched in 1906. The new vessel gave its name to a class of ship and the Germans soon built some of their own. By 1914, they had thirteen dreadnoughts, but the British kept their supremacy with twenty-four.

Just before the outbreak of war, the main British fleet moved to Scapa Flow, off the Orkney Islands, to take control of the North Sea. In late 1914, German ships shelled towns on Britain's east coast, including Scarborough. However, the ships were chased away by British battle cruisers. They returned to their own ports and did not venture out again until the Battle of Jutland (see page 27). This was not only because the British were keeping them away—the Kaiser did not want to risk the costly dreadnoughts in an all-out battle.

Keeping the German fleet in port was part of a wider naval blockade. The Royal Navy stopped and inspected all ships from neutral countries, confiscating food or raw materials bound for Germany. The Germans began to suffer serious shortages and introduced rationing. In February 1915, they struck back by beginning submarine warfare.

German submarines, known as U-boats, aimed to impose a counter-blockade. It was difficult for underwater vessels to stop and search ships, so the U-boats planned to sink them without warning. For this reason, Germany declared its intention to attack only enemy, not neutral, ships. However, when a U-boat torpedoed the British ship *Lusitania* on May 7, 1915, 128 American passengers drowned. This led to wide protest in the United States, and President Woodrow Wilson threatened war.

Germany could not risk the United States joining the Allies. With just twenty-two submarines, Germany could never make the counter-blockade fully effective. So Germany changed its strategy. U-boats began to surface in order to inspect ships in the blockade zone, seizing cargoes when it was considered necessary. However, German methods changed again in 1917 (see pages 40–41).

In this photograph, which dates from 1916, German sailors stand on top of a U-boat that has surfaced. In 1917, the U-boat campaign increased dramatically (see page 40).

During the First World War, Martin Niemöller served on German U-boats. He later became a Protestant minister who made a stand against Adolf Hitler and spent World War II in a concentration camp. This description of a U-boat attack in the spring of 1916 appears in his autobiography *From U-boat to Concentration Camp* (1939).

U-boats were fitted with deck guns.

Inverlyon is the name of the ship that the U-boat had stopped.

 The German government placed this advertisement in the *New York World* newspaper on May 1, 1915, the day the *Lusitania* set sail from the U.S. Few passengers believed that Germany would plan to hit a passenger liner. A total of twelve hundred people died when the ship was hit six days later.

THE BATTLE OF JUTLAND

The dreadnoughts met in one major battle, which was triggered by the actions of German naval chief Admiral Reinhard Scheer. On May 31, 1916, Scheer sent battle cruisers to the seas off Jutland, a Danish peninsula. He hoped that the British would send ships of the same size in response. German dreadnoughts would then steam in to destroy the British vessels. However, the Royal Navy learned of Scheer's plans. It sent battle cruisers from Rosyth, as he was expecting. But it also sent dreadnoughts from Scapa Flow. The six-hour battle that followed was indecisive, but afterward the German dreadnoughts returned to their ports for good.

Hove to means "came to a stop."

...on the afternoon of the 11th [April], we approached a large sailing vessel, which **hove to** at our warning shot, her crew taking to the boats, while we tried to sink her by **gunfire**. It was a difficult job, as the sea kept breaking right over the gun's crew, and... Seaman Pehrson was washed overboard when his lifebelt carried away. All attempts to pick him up... failed... When the **Inverlyon** was finally sunk, after a couple of dozen hits, none of us could rejoice at this first success.

The sinking of the *Lusitania*

Travellers intending to embark on the Atlantic voyage are reminded that a state of war exists between Germany and her allies; that the zone of war includes the waters adjacent to the British Isles; that, in accordance with formal notice given by the Imperial German Government, vessels flying the flag of Great Britain, or of any of her allies, are liable to destruction in those waters and that travellers sailing in the war zone on ships of Great Britain or her allies do so at their own risk.

THE HOME FRONTS

Civilian life was disrupted by World War I, and people had no choice but to adapt. They believed that they were fighting for victory, not on the Eastern and Western battlefronts, but on the home front.

Much of civilian life in Britain was controlled by the Defense of the Realm Act (DORA), passed on August 8, 1914. It granted the government emergency powers, such as taking over factories for munitions production, growing crops on private land, and increasing work hours. Taxes were raised to fund the fighting, and food rationing was introduced in 1918.

Many French civilians had to endure even worse conditions, since about 12 percent of their land was either occupied or in use as a battlefield. In addition, conscription meant that almost every man between the ages of eighteen and forty-seven was away at the front. As in Britain,

British civilians line up to receive mutton stew, puddings, and other food at this communal kitchen in Hammersmith, London, in 1917.

serious food supply problems began in 1917. Rationing, introduced in 1914, grew ever more strict, and prices soared.

In Germany, conscription sent millions of men to the trenches in 1914. Once the German government realized the conflict would not be over quickly, it mobilized the civilian population for war, too. Much of this workforce produced arms and ammunition.

Germany experienced food shortages almost from the start of the war. Rationing began in 1915. By the winter of 1916, people in Germany were starving. Forced employment, hunger, and military failure changed the character of the German home front, as early patriotism turned to bitterness.

In Russia, lack of food, harsh conditions in munitions factories, and humiliation in battle also led to serious unrest. Czar Nicholas II and his wife Alexandra were unable to deal

Heavy guns in production at the giant Krupp Works in Essen, Germany (see page 9).

with the problems. Revolution and an early withdrawal from the war followed.

Despite the neutrality of the United States, the war also affected American life. The American Red Cross mobilized American civilians to assist on the battlefields of France. The Red Cross also sent a mercy ship to France to provide assistance to soldiers of all nationalities. In the United States, the decline in immigrants from war-torn Europe caused a labor shortage in northern industries. This presented opportunities for African-Americans, who moved north in large numbers during the war.

TOTAL WAR

Until 1914, wars were usually confined to battlefields. Though changed, life elsewhere in the participating countries was not completely transformed. World War I was different. Civilian workers produced deadly armaments on a huge scale. Governments and, especially in Germany, the army took control of daily life. Air raids (see pages 36–37) brought the conflict to the home fronts, and high death rates in battle left almost every family in mourning. German general Erich Ludendorff coined a term for this new phenomenon: total war.

In this second excerpt from his autobiography, Robert Graves (see page 19) describes the effects of rationing on his London wedding.

Nancy and I were married in January 1918 at St James's Church, Piccadilly… At this stage of the war, sugar could not be got except in the form of rations. There was a three-tiered wedding-cake and the Nicholsons had been saving up their **sugar and butter cards** for a month to make it taste like a real one; but when George Mallory lifted off the plaster-case of imitation icing, a sigh of disappointment rose from the guests.

The government issued people with ration books. They contained coupons that were detached by the shop-owner every time a purchase was made. They could also be used in restaurants.

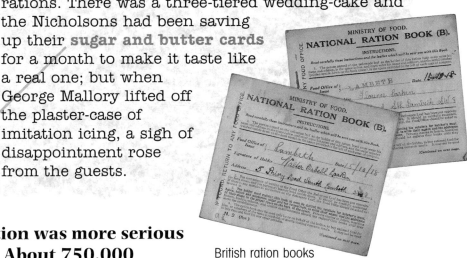

British ration books

In Germany, the situation was more serious than in Great Britain. About 750,000 Germans died of starvation during the war. Evelyn, Princess Blücher (see page 13), wrote this account of hunger on the German home front.

Germans lining up for food in 1915

KRIEBLOWITZ, January 1917.—We are all growing thinner every day, and the rounded contours of the German nation have become a legend of the past. We are all gaunt and bony now, and have dark shadows round our eyes, and our thoughts are chiefly taken up with wondering what our next meal will be, and dreaming of the good things that once existed.

WOMEN AT WAR

This French magazine dates from 1916. The cover illustration contrasts hat-making and other light work done by women before the war with heavy industrial work that they undertook during the war.

Women's lives changed tremendously during World War I. Many took on traditional male roles at home, while some ventured into war zones.

Before the war, about 25 percent of Britain's 23.7 million women worked outside the home. Most of the rest were full-time wives and mothers. However, as men went to fight, and especially after conscription began in 1916, women filled the jobs that soldiers left behind. They also took on new jobs created by the demands of war. Women worked in munitions factories, as well as in a wide range of other occupations, from printer to bus conductor. Many also joined the Women's

Land Army, founded in 1916, and spent the war on the nation's farms.

Thousands of British women went out to the fronts. Some, mainly from the upper classes, belonged to the First Aid Nursing Yeomanry (FANY). Most of its members served as ambulance drivers. Women who enrolled in the Voluntary Aid Detachment (VAD) carried out a great variety of duties, from nursing with the Red Cross to cooking. In 1917, the government set up branches of the army, navy, and air force for women, but their members did not take part in combat.

French women worked in factories, fields, and offices throughout the war. By mid-1915, thirty thousand women were making munitions in France. In 1916, a new law forbade employers to hire men for jobs that women could do. A Committee on Female

Many British women worked as wartime bus conductors.

Labor was also established to monitor women's working conditions. French women also served as nurses, at home and on the battlefield.

Germany did not allow women at the front. However, at home they worked at almost everything, from the production of ammunition to building an underground train system in Berlin. The National Women's Service League organized nurseries to look after children while women worked.

Women in the United States also participated in the war, even before U.S. soldiers began fighting. In August 1914, a contingent of 255 American Red Cross nurses arrived in France to staff a surgical hospital. When the Red Cross ran out of money for their salaries, communities around the country raised money so they could stay.

EDITH CAVELL

In 1914, English nurse Edith Cavell was matron of a Red Cross hospital in Brussels. When the Germans occupied the city during their invasion of Belgium, she helped Allied soldiers escape into neutral Holland. The Germans caught her and sentenced her to death. Before she was killed by firing squad in October 1915, she said: "Standing, as I do, in the view of God and eternity, I realize that patriotism is not enough. I must have no hatred or bitterness towards anyone." She became a national heroine and helped to alter people's view of women at war.

Edith Cavell in the garden of her Brussels home in 1915

Maria Botchkareva, known as Yashka, was allowed to join the Russian army in 1914. In 1917, she set up the all-female "Battalion of Death." This excerpt from her autobiography, *Yashka: My Life as Peasant, Exile, and Soldier* (1919), describes some incidents from the unit's early days.

I marched the recruits to four barbers' shops, where... a number of barbers cut short the hair of one woman after another... The same afternoon my soldiers received their first lessons... and the drilling went on without interference. Giggling was strictly forbidden... One day... Mrs. Pankhurst was introduced to me, and I ordered the Battalion to salute the eminent visitor who had done so much for women and her country. Mrs Pankhurst became a frequent visitor to the Battalion, watching it with deep interest as it grew into a well-disciplined military unit.

Mrs Emmeline Pankhurst was a leader of the British "Votes for Women" campaign.

Maria Botchkareva

CHAPTER 4

1916

VERDUN

In 1916, battles on the Western Front reached new levels of horror. The first major offensive was launched by the Germans against the French.

Erich von Falkenhayn (see page 16) planned the new attack, code named *Gericht*. His goal was to crush the spirit of the French army. For this reason, he chose Verdun as the battle site—the capture of its forts had been a major blow to the French in the 1870–71 war (see page 9). He figured that if France collapsed, Britain would choose to start peace negotiations rather than continue alone.

Meanwhile, the French commander, General Joffre, was planning a joint Franco-British attack on the Somme (see pages 34–35). So while Germany was preparing a force of 140,000 for the Verdun offensive, French troops and guns were moving away. Despite warnings, Joffre refused to recognize Verdun's importance or strengthen its defenses.

The devastating German attack began on February 21. Howitzers and other artillery rained down shells. As the German soldiers advanced, they unleashed phosgene gas and used flamethrowers for the first time. On February 25, they captured Fort Douaumont, near Verdun, in three-quarters of an hour.

At this time of crisis, Joffre called on General Henri Philippe Pétain for assistance. Pétain took control at Verdun, stating: "They [the Germans] shall not pass." Then he began to turn his downcast, freezing troops into a defensive machine. Soon the French artillery was responding to heavy German attacks with equal force. Pétain also improved the only French supply route, the so-called "Sacred Way."

THE WESTERN FRONT 1916–17

Members of a small French artillery unit at Verdun. Their quick-firing gun launched huge shells toward enemy lines.

Von Falkenhayn matched Pétain's determination, and the fighting spun out of control. The Germans captured Fort Vaux, about 2 miles (3 km) from Verdun, on June 7. However, as they moved toward the town itself, thousands of German troops had to leave for Russia (see box). Soon after, the British attacked on the Somme River, diverting more German resources. Von Falkenhayn had missed his opportunity.

The fighting continued, but with less intensity. Paul von Hindenburg replaced von Falkenhayn in August. In October, a French offensive recaptured Forts Douaumont and Vaux. By December, the front had returned almost to its original position, and the toll of dead and wounded was nearly one million.

THE BRUSILOV OFFENSIVE

By 1916, the Russian army had regrouped after the disastrous retreat of the previous year (see page 25). Its commanders planned an attack in July, to coincide with the Allied offensive on the Somme. But by June, France was in trouble at Verdun, and Italy was under pressure on its Austro-Hungarian border. Both asked Russia for help. So on June 4, General Alexei Brusilov launched surprise attacks against the Austrian army on the Eastern Front. The Austrians were driven back, but the Germans came to their aid. Romania, which joined the Allies in August, tried to help Russia, but was quickly defeated by Germany. By September, Russia had retreated and lost one million men.

Verdun was the longest battle of World War I. About forty million artillery shells were fired as one attack followed after another. Henri Desagneaux served as a commander in the front line for two weeks. Here he describes the events of June 17.

An **ammunition dump** was a place where ammunition was stored.

One cannot imagine what the simple phrase of an official statement like "We have recaptured a trench" really means! The attack is prepared from 4 to 9 o'clock; all guns firing together. The Germans fire non-stop, **ammunition dumps** blow up... The wounded from this morning's attack are beginning to arrive, we learn what happened: our artillery fired too short and demolished our front line trench...When we attacked the Germans let us advance to 15 meters [16.5 yards] and then caught us in a hail of machine-gunfire. We succeeded in capturing several parts of the trench but couldn't hold them... At nightfall, the dead arrive on stretchers at the cemetery... Major Payen, his head red with blood; Major Cormouls, black with smoke, still others unrecognizable and often in pieces.

THE SOMME

By July 1916, the date of the Somme offensive, France was in deep trouble at Verdun. As a result, it could not send the agreed forty troop divisions to the new battleground. Instead it sent five, while Britain initially supplied fourteen. But General Sir Douglas Haig (see page 25) still believed that an all-out "push" would produce the needed break in the German lines.

General Haig believed in offensive warfare and in the power of mounted troops. He planned to use both on the Somme, pushing infantry (foot soldiers) forward until the enemy cracked, then sending in cavalry. In fact, such nineteenth-century tactics were no match for twentieth-century military technology.

The British soldiers, many of them inexperienced volunteers, faced a daunting task. The Germans were on high ground, so they could defend their lines

British painter Paul Nash became a soldier in 1914 and an official war artist in 1916. His painting of trench warfare in winter is called *Over the Top*. Nash was also an official artist in World War II.

relatively easily. They also had a good view of enemy activity below. The German trenches were solidly built with deep dugouts that protected troops during attacks.

The British began their attack on June 23 and pounded the Germans with artillery for a week. The goal was to destroy the German front-line trenches and barbed wire before the advance. However, the guns could not wipe out the Germans' deep dugouts, and shrapnel shells were ineffective against the barbed wire. Nevertheless, the infantry attack began on July 1.

As the lines of British soldiers went over the top, German machine gunners, sheltered in dugouts, mowed them down. The German artillery joined the battle, too. Soon No Man's Land was

strewn with bodies and injured men crying out in pain. About 120,000 men attacked on that first day. At the day's end, about twenty thousand were dead; forty thousand were wounded, missing, or taken prisoner.

Haig forged ahead with his plan in spite of the heavy losses, and the number of deaths grew. Germans fell in the thousands, too. On September 15, the Allies used tanks in battle for the first time. Some broke down. Others moved so slowly that the Germans could target them easily. An Allied attack in November failed, and the battle wound down. Total casualties in the Somme were over one million; about 60 per cent were Allied troops. Britain had won about 7 1/2 miles (12 km) of land.

General Sir Douglas Haig

Captain R.J. Trousdell of the Royal Irish Fusiliers wrote this description of the Somme battle area.

In the open, no sign of vegetation was visible: shell craters literally overlapped over square miles—gashes in the torn surface, more or less continuous and deeper than the rest—indicated trenches, and in these our troops managed to exist, shelled day and night until they went forward to the attack or were replaced by other troops... Thickly timbered woods were reduced to a few gaunt and splintered trunks. Stripped of every leaf and twig—without undergrowth—almost without roots. Villages disappeared as though they had never been...

Shells have just about destroyed these woods on the Somme battlefield.

Many Australians fought on the Somme. In this poem, Australian soldier Vance Palmer writes about his inability to forget the experience.

Airplanes flew over the battlefield (see pages 36–7).

Will they never fade or pass—
The mud, and the misty figures endlessly coming
In file through the foul morass,
And the grey flood-water lipping the reeds and grass,
And the **steel wings drumming**?

...
I have returned to these;
The farm, and kindly Bush, and the young calves lowing;
But all that my mind sees
Is a quaking bog in a mist—stark, snapped trees,
And the **dark Somme flowing.**

The Somme area is named after the river that runs through it.

THE MILITARY SERVICE ACT

Until 1916, the British army consisted of regular (career) soldiers and the three million volunteers recruited by Lord Kitchener (see page 17). However, heavy losses meant that many more men were needed. So in January 1916, the Military Service Act was passed. It introduced conscription—compulsory military service—for single men between the ages of eighteen and forty-one. In May, married men were called up, too. The age limit was also gradually raised to fifty. Some men were exempt from conscription. They included conscientious objectors, who often faced hostility and imprisonment.

THE WAR IN THE AIR

British observers in a kite balloon watch enemy activity on the Western Front. Kite balloons were tied to the ground, but could rise to 1.1 miles (1800 m).

Both the Allies and the Central Powers used aircraft from the very beginning of World War I. It was not until later that airplanes began to play a major role in the fighting, however.

At the start of the war, airplanes were sent out to detect enemy troops' movement and trench locations. Ground forces used information from aerial observers to target their guns. To that point, no military leader had thought of planes as fighting machines.

Change came after both sides sent up airplanes to shoot down reconnaissance aircraft. Pilots fixed machine guns on their planes in order to attack the enemy. When guns fired straight ahead, however, there was a risk of hitting the propellers. In 1915, Frenchman Roland Garros invented a device to make the guns fire only when propellers were turned away. When the Germans shot down Garros, designer Anthony Fokker improved the invention. After German planes were fitted with the new "interrupter gear," the Allies made their own interrupter system.

From 1915 on, fighter planes armed with this new technology engaged in sky duels over the trenches. The era of the daredevil flying aces had begun.

Air tactics changed as the war continued and as better planes were developed. Allied squadrons sought to keep certain areas clear of enemy aircraft by mounting regular patrols. German squadrons operated the "circus system," moving to wherever the need was greatest. Formation-fighting took over from individual combat, and planes began to attack ground targets, such as trenches.

Beginning in 1914, Aircraft was also used to bomb areas far from the fronts. German Zeppelin airships attacked civilian targets

This painting shows an aerial dogfight between German and British biplanes. The German aircraft are marked with black crosses, the British with red, white and blue bull's-eye symbols.

in Britain, France, and elsewhere. Raids were less frequent after 1916, as the Allies began to shoot down the hydrogen-filled ships with incendiary bullets. Starting in 1917, Allied bombers regularly attacked factories and mines in Germany, while German Gotha bombers raided British cities. By 1918, aircraft was recognized as a powerful means of waging war.

THE ROYAL AIR FORCE

When the war began, Britain had two airborne fighting forces. The Royal Flying Corps was part of the army and the Royal Naval Air Service part of the navy. As the importance of airpower increased, the need for change became clear. Major General Sir Hugh Trenchard, head of the Royal Flying Corps, did not want the army to lose control of its air force. But he was persuaded to take on the task of creating a unified service. The Royal Air Force was formed in April 1918.

Searchlights pick out a huge German Zeppelin as it prepares to bomb the British mainland during a nighttime raid.

The German "Red Baron" (see document) was the most successful flying ace. He shot down eighty planes before he was brought down in 1918.

The "Red Baron," Manfred von Richthofen, was so called because his Fokker plane was painted red. During the war, von Richthofen kept a diary. It was published after his death, with a selection of his letters. This excerpt is taken from one of the letters.

Before Verdun, 3 May 1916
Very sincere thanks for your kind wishes on my birthday, which I spent very pleasantly here. In the morning I had three very nerve-wracking aerial combats, and in the evening I sat with Zeumer, my first pilot, until one o'clock in the morning with a bowl of punch under a blossoming apple tree. I feel very content with my new occupation as a fighter pilot; I believe that no post in the war is as attractive as this one.

The full name of the British pilot who wrote this excerpt is not known. Dated August 1917, his view of the war in the air is quite different from that of the Red Baron (above).

The flying job is rotten for one's nerve, and although one is supposed to last 6 months with a fortnight's leave half way, quite a lot of people's nerve completely conks out after 4 or 4½... No one can imagine the strain of 2½ hours over the line. Firstly one has to keep one's place in the formation... then one has to watch the leader, who does all the scientific dodging of **Archie**... Then there's every single machine in the sky to be suspicious about, until you've proved it isn't a **Hun**.

Archie is slang for anti-aircraft gunfire from the ground.

Hun is a derogatory word for "German."

PROPAGANDA AND CENSORSHIP

Propaganda (biased information designed to support a particular cause) and censorship (the suppression of information) were widely used during World War I. Governments, armies, and the media on both sides relied more and more on these machines as the conflict progressed.

Propaganda began with the war. Newspapers and the general public spread rumors that enemy troops had committed evil atrocities, such as cutting off dead soldiers' feet. Enemy incompetence was another favorite topic. The French press announced that German shells were made of cardboard. At the same time, people glorified their own troops' bravery. The troops themselves were not impressed by such stories. Troops at the fronts often felt closer to their enemies nearby, who knew the truth, than to misinformed people at home.

The nature of government news censorship varied from country to country. The War Press Office in Germany exercised strict control, enforced by the army. The French authorities did not permit the lists of war dead and wounded to be published, but provided rose-tinted stories of their own. In Britain, a member of Lord Kitchener's staff wrote the official war reports. Kitchener then had to approve them before they were sent out to the newspapers. From May 1915,

Beat back the HUN with LIBERTY BONDS

This poster advertises Liberty Bonds, certificates of debt sold by the American government to pay for the war. By showing an evil-looking German (Hun) soldier, it also acts as anti-German propaganda.

some British journalists were allowed to join troops at the front and send reports home.

The propaganda war increased in 1916, when film took on an important role. A film called *The Battle of the Somme* was made on the battlefield while the fighting was still under way. Its scenes of brave British troops were meant to encourage the public at home. However, many people were shocked by the violence—even though it did not come close to grim reality. German commander Erich Ludendorff supported the making of propaganda news films from 1917. They showed sympathetic images of Germany's troops at the fronts and people flocked to watch them.

British comedy actor Charlie Chaplin starred in a silent propaganda film called *Shoulder Arms* (1918). In it, he won the war on his own!

This letter, dated 1916, was written by a British soldier. Information that might have been of use to the enemy has been crossed out by the censor.

THE HINDENBURG CULT

An unusual propaganda plan was developed by German military officials to cover up the failure of the Schlieffen Plan (see page 12). Playing on the public's wish to idolize its soldiers, they encouraged the hero-worship of a particular military leader. This was Paul von Hindenburg, one of the commanders responsible for German victory at Tannenberg (see page 14).

A huge statue of Hindenburg was built in Berlin's Tiergarten park. People paid for the privilege of hitting nails into the statue. This was supposed to make Hindenburg an even stronger "Iron Man." The money helped to pay for the war.

Crowds flock around the statue of Hindenburg in Berlin, while a military band plays to entertain them.

Propaganda leaflets dropped by airplanes over the trenches were designed to demoralize the enemy. These leaflets often informed troops that defeat was imminent and resistance useless. This is the text of a leaflet that the Germans dropped over American lines in 1918, a year after the United States joined the Allies.

NEVER SAY DIE!
Don't die until you have to!
What business have you to die for France, for Alsace-Lorraine, or for England in France?
Isn't it better anyhow to live than to die, no matter for how "glorious" a cause? Isn't it better to live and come back to the old folks at home, than to rot in the shell holes and trenches of France?
If you surrender to us, we will treat you fair enough.
Why run any more chances than you have to?
You might as well be a free boarder in Germany till the war is over.
YOU DON'T WANT TO DIE TILL YOU HAVE TO!

CHAPTER 5

1917
ENTER THE UNITED STATES

The great Western Front confrontations of 1916—Verdun and the Somme—had no real winners. They were classic battles of attrition in which each side tried to win simply by inflicting high casualties on the other. By 1917, it was clear that this strategy had failed. Erich Ludendorff, who was now in charge of the German armed forces with Paul von Hindenburg, changed tactics in the trenches. He also decided that the war could only be won at sea.

On January 31, 1917, Germany declared all-out submarine warfare. All ships in the Atlantic war zone, neutral and as Allied, were to be sunk. With this extreme measure, Germany hoped to starve Britain, force the Allies into peace negotiations, and bring the war to a speedy end. Success was likely because Germany had many more U-boats—well over two hundred—than it had in 1915.

U.S. president Woodrow Wilson, angered by Germany's move, immediately broke off diplomatic relations. However, he still wanted to continue the popular U.S. policy of neutrality. Wilson spent much of 1916 leading negotiations to bring "peace without victory." In November, as a result of his efforts, the Central Powers agreed to undertake peace negotiations. Allied countries were skeptical, as peace terms at that time would have likely favored the Central Powers.

Wilson's failure, coupled with increased U-boat attacks, brought the United States to the brink of war. Then, in January 1917, British code specialists intercepted a telegram from German foreign minister Arthur Zimmerman to the German minister to Mexico. Zimmerman offered Mexico the right to reclaim Texas, New Mexico, and Arizona in

This idealistic illustration of soldiers leaving for the war appeared on the cover of an American children's magazine in 1918.

President Woodrow Wilson reads the U.S. declaration of war to Congress on April 6, 1917.

American troops land at SI-Nazaire on the French coast in June 1917.

THE U.S. ARMY

Before it entered the war, the U.S. Army had only about 200,000 soldiers. By the end of the conflict, about two million Americans, including 200,000 African-Americans, were serving in Europe. They brought little experience of trench warfare to the fronts and were largely dependent on the other Allies for weapons and equipment. However, they made a major contribution to the Allied victory (see pages 52–53).

return for joining the Central Powers. On March 1, U.S. newspapers published news of the telegram, causing a nationwide tide of anger toward Germany. On April 6, 1917, the U.S. Congress declared war.

Passed in May, the Selective Service Act required all American men aged 21 to 30 to join the armed forces (the age range later became 18 to 45). The American Expeditionary Force, under General John Pershing, entered France in June.

Meanwhile, the U-boat campaign was taking its toll. By spring 1917, the Germans were destroying about eight hundred vessels each month. Britain's food supplies were dwindling fast. Prime Minister David Lloyd George devised a plan: merchant ships were to travel in groups of about forty, flanked by warship escorts. Over the next six months, only twenty-four out of fifteen hundred ships bound for England were sunk.

This excerpt comes from a letter written by Sergeant Phelps Harding, whose 306th Infantry Regiment formed part of the American Expeditionary Force.

Camp Upton, NY, 29 March, 1918

Dear Dad,

I just wrote Mother that the regiment is almost ready to leave for France... This letter is addressed to you... to avoid Mother seeing it. I simply want to tell you that we were secretly... practically given our preference as to whether we would rather serve here or abroad... Don't tell Mother that I had an opportunity to stay here, for I know that it would make her feel badly that I did not stay. I am just telling you so that if anything should happen to me you will know that I met the danger of my own free will, and with a full knowledge of what to expect in the fighting on the other side. I'm mighty glad I have the chance to go over and do my share —and I know you are glad to have me go...

THE NIVELLE OFFENSIVE

In December 1916, General Robert Nivelle replaced General Joffre as the French Chief of Staff. Nivelle planned to launch a new Allied offensive in 1917 that would finally break the Western Front stalemate.

Erich Ludendorff had decided on an entirely different strategy. He had already put Germany on the *offensive* at sea (see pages 40–41). On the Western Front he wanted to strengthen Germany's *defensive* position. So troops were ordered to withdraw 19 miles (about 30 km) to the east and build the Hindenburg Line (see map, page 32). A complex system of barbed wire, machine-gun positions, and dugouts stretched for many miles along the line and up to 10 miles (16 km) back from it. Its purpose was to keep the enemy at bay.

Nivelle's offensive was planned to begin in Champagne

The Germans spent months building strong, deep trenches like this along the Hindenburg Line. Troops withdrew to the line in March 1917.

in mid-April. On April 9, the British, Canadians, and Australians launched a smaller attack at Arras, to the north. The plan was to keep the Germans busy while the main preparations continued elsewhere. At first all went according to plan. The Allies advanced about 3 miles (5 km), and the Canadians captured the area of high ground known as Vimy Ridge. But the Germans fought back strongly, and the battle wound down on May 17.

The main attack, launched on April 16, took place in an area known as the Chemin des Dames, near Rheims. But the Germans had learned about the French plan ahead of time from a captured soldier and were fully prepared. During the first two days of the offensive, French soldiers advanced into a torrent of machine-gun bullets. It was soon clear that no breakthrough was possible, but Nivelle continued the attack. After two weeks, the French had advanced about a third of a mile (half a

Canadian troops move toward Vimy Ridge. They were led by General Sir Julian Byng, who later became governor general of Canada.

kilometer). Casualty figures had reached 250,000.

The pointless slaughter and Nivelle's persistence (the offensive continued into May) led to a protest by French troops. Reserves who were supposed to move to the front lines refused to move, and front-line troops refused to attack. Eventually about half a million men joined the protest. Calm returned when Nivelle was replaced by General Pétain. He promised the troops an end to huge, unwinnable offensives, reminded them that American help was on the way, and improved the conditions in which they lived and fought.

British soldiers prepare for the Battle of Arras. The men at the front observe the enemy using a periscope and binoculars. The others are passing information on to troops elsewhere using a field telephone.

In Arras, Allied troops extended an existing cave system under the city to provide shelter and a way of reaching German lines without exposing themselves to gunfire. Brigadier General Douglas, Lord Loch, wrote this account of the caves.

The old French built their towns by quarrying down till they came to the hard chalk and then dug it out. This has made huge caves. We joined them up and made entrances etc. Lit them by electric light. Made cook houses—Divisional and Brigade headquarters etc., etc. On the day of the attack you could walk underground from the centre of Arras to the German front line. The last 150 feet we blew out at **zero hour**. We consequently had communication trenches across No Man's Land in under half an hour.

Zero hour means the hour when the attack began.

PRISONERS OF WAR

The soldier who revealed the Nivelle Offensive details to the Germans was one of about eight million prisoners captured in World War I. After an attack, captured men were usually put into cages, then moved to prison camps. After a period of interrogation, they were often sent out to work on farms and other places. Conditions were poor. On the Eastern Front, many prisoners caught typhoid.

This illustration dates from 1917 and shows German prisoners behind the barbed wire fence of a French prisoner-of-war camp.

PASSCHENDAELE

The French protest came to an end in June. As Pétain had promised, France did not launch any more major attacks during World War I. However, Haig began to argue that one last, British-led push could defeat the Germans. The location that he favored for the attempt was Ypres (see pages 16 and 24–25).

Ypres was in a salient—a bulge in the front line surrounded by enemy-held land. Despite the difficulty of attacking in such an area, Haig wanted to break out of the salient and push ahead to the Belgian ports that the Germans were using as submarine bases. British prime minister Lloyd George had

serious doubts about the plan. However, Haig pointed out that the German forces were weaker than in the past, while the British had new weapons, aircraft, and tanks, better battle techniques, and more accurate aerial photographs.

On June 7, 1917, before the main attack began, Allied troops led by General Sir Herbert Plumer used underground mines to seize the Messines Ridge. This was an area of high ground near Ypres that gave the Germans a clear view of the enemy. The operation was brilliantly executed, but instead of moving swiftly to take advantage of German confusion, the Allies waited seven weeks before launching the offensive.

The Third Battle of Ypres began on July 31, 1917. A heavy rain soon began to fall, and the preliminary attack—the biggest yet—hurled over 4.5 million shells into the muddy battleground. Troops moved through a swamp. Progress was slow throughout August, and losses were heavy. However, during a dry spell in September, Anzac and British troops captured Menin Road Ridge, Polygon Wood, and Broodseinde.

Torrential rain fell again in October, and men and horses

Stretcher-bearers in the mud at Passchendaele in 1917. Torrential rain turned the battlefield into a lethal quagmire.

drowned in the mud. Despite the conditions, troops pushed on. Canadians took the village of Passchendaele on November 6. Haig then stopped the offensive. The Allies had advanced about 6 miles (10 km) into the salient, leaving themselves more exposed. Over 400,000 had died. Reeling from the worst defeat to date, men began to lose all hope.

The Battle of Cambrai, which began about 50 miles (80 km) south of Ypres on November 28, gave the Allies a small boost. About four hundred tanks of a new type known as Mark IV smashed through German lines and advanced about 5 miles (8 km). However, the Germans quickly regained the ground.

A Mark IV tank in action at Cambrai. The battle was such a success for the Allies that church bells in London were rung to celebrate.

The Battle of Passchendaele was a disaster. However, in his papers Field Marshal Haig recalls that he received the following congratulatory telegram from the British government on October 16, 1917.

The War Cabinet desire to congratulate you and the troops under your command upon the achievements of the British Armies in Flanders in the great battle which has been raging since July 31st. Starting from positions in which every advantage rested with the enemy and, hampered and delayed from time to time by most unfavorable weather, you and your men have nevertheless continuously driven the enemy back with such skill, courage, and **pertinacity**, as have commanded the grateful admiration of the peoples of the British Empire and filled the enemy with alarm...

Pertinacity means "determination."

THE BATTLE OF CAPORETTO

Italy had been struggling against the Austro-Hungarians on its border since 1915 (see page 25). Much of the fighting took place in the Alps. The two sides were evenly balanced, and by 1917 neither had achieved a decisive victory. Then Erich Ludendorff sent in German troops to help the Austro-Hungarians, and a joint attack was launched at Caporetto on October 24. Italy suffered a major defeat, and its army retreated more than 62 miles (100 km). British and French troops rushed to the rescue.

EXIT RUSSIA

World War I had put Russia's armies to shame. They had been crushed at Tannenberg in 1914, driven out of Poland in 1915, and forced to retreat after the Brusilov Offensive of 1916. There was no comfort at home, where food shortages were leading to starvation, inflation was soaring, and industrial unrest was increasing.

Czar Nicholas II had already survived one revolution—in 1905. In March 1917, he was under the gun again. Women lining up for food in Russia's capital, Petrograd (now St. Petersburg), began to riot. The unrest spread, and protesters took to the streets. The czar ordered the army to shoot into

THE EASTERN FRONT 1917–18

Area occupied under Treaty of Brest-Litovsk, March 1918

Armistice Line

0   200 miles
0   300 km

Baltic Sea • Riga • Moscow • GERMANY • Brest-Litovsk • Warsaw • POLAND • Failed Russian offensive 1917 • Kiev • RUSSIA • Dnieper River • UKRAINE • GALICIA • AUSTRIA-HUNGARY • Odessa • CRIMEA • ROMANIA • Black Sea

Czar Nicholas II with three of his daughters. He, his wife Alexandra, and their five children were all executed by revolutionaries on July 16, 1918.

the crowds. However, many soldiers simply refused to fire.

The czar now realized that change was inevitable. He set up a provisional government, headed by Prince Lvov, to take control of the country. Then, on March 17, he abdicated—gave up all power. Prince Lvov and his ministers had to decide whether Russia should withdraw from the war. The provisional government did not want to abandon its allies, so it chose to continue.

Soldiers were now even more reluctant to fight. Many began to support the revolutionaries who were campaigning for an immediate end to the war. These men had set up workers' committees, known as *soviets*, all across the country, and their power was growing. The Germans decided to exploit this

situation. They allowed Vladimir Lenin, leader of the revolutionary Bolshevik Party, to return to Russia. He traveled by train from Switzerland through Germany, arriving home in April.

The situation grew steadily worse for the provisional government. In June its new leader, Alexander Kerensky, ordered an offensive against Germany. It was a total failure and German troops advanced east. The Petrograd soviet, headed by Lenin's fellow Bolshevik, Leon Trotsky, believed that the time had come to seize power. On November 6, Trotsky launched the revolution. Bolshevik forces took over the city and the government fled.

Lenin became leader of the new Russia and began talks with Germany to end his country's participation in World War I. The cease-fire began on December 3, 1917. Leon Trotsky, now foreign minister, began to negotiate the terms of peace. The Treaty of Brest-Litovsk, signed in March 1918, brought more humiliation to Russia. It was forced to sign away vast areas of land (see map, page 46).

In this scene from the 1917 revolution, Bolsheviks in Petrograd aim their rifles at government supporters.

VLADIMIR LENIN

Vladimir Ilyich Lenin studied law and while still a young man became a follower of the German philosopher Karl Marx. The Russian government punished him for spreading Marxist political ideas by sending him to Siberia in 1895. He was released in 1900, and five years later played an

important part in the 1905 revolution. After its failure he was exiled to Switzerland, where he remained until the Germans returned him to Russia in 1917. Lenin ruled his country from the revolution until his death in 1924. His tomb is in Moscow's Red Square.

Lenin was a powerful speaker, as this Russian poster illustrates. He used his charisma to spread Communist ideas.

 This is part of a speech that Lenin made to the Petrograd soviet on the day that the Bolsheviks seized the city.

Lenin is referring to the revolutions of 1905, March 1917, and November 1917.

Lenin believed in Marx's theory of revolutionary socialism. It teaches that the working class should overthrow the capitalist system, in which industry is privately owned, and replace it with a new system based on common ownership.

Proletarian means "working class."

From now on, a new phase in the history of Russia begins, and this, **the third Russian revolution**, should in the end lead to the **victory of socialism**. One of our urgent tasks is to put an immediate end to the war... We shall be helped in this by the world working-class movement, which is already beginning to develop in Italy, Britain and Germany. The proposal we make to international democracy for a just and immediate peace will everywhere awaken an ardent response among the international **proletarian** masses.

WAR IN THE MIDDLE EAST

Gallipoli (see pages 22–23) was not the only place where the Allies and Turks fought. They also clashed in Palestine and Mesopotamia (now Iraq), both of which were then part of the Ottoman Empire. In 1917, as Russia was preparing to withdraw from the war, Allied activity in the Middle East increased. This was because the Allies were afraid that Turkish troops who had been fighting the Russians would now move to the Middle East.

The Allied interest in Palestine stemmed from their wish to protect the Suez Canal, a vital shipping link that cuts through Egypt to connect the Mediterranean and Red Seas. The Turks attacked the canal in 1915. Throughout 1916, the British steadily pushed them back into Palestine, but were unable to defeat them completely. In early 1917, two more British attacks failed. Britain sent General Sir Edmund Allenby to lead a new offensive in June of the same year. The appointment was successful. The Palestinian towns of Gaza and Beersheba fell in October. Jerusalem surrendered on December 9.

Allenby's offensive was backed by Arabs who wanted to throw off Turkish rule. They were led by Emir Feisal ibn Hussein, whose father was the

PALESTINE AND MESOPOTAMIA

General Sir Edmund Allenby

sherif (governor) of Mecca. Feisal was supported by British army intelligence officer T.E. Lawrence, now known as Lawrence of Arabia (see document, page 49). The two men organized the Arabs into highly effective guerrilla units that pounded the Turks.

The British landed in Mesopotamia in November 1914. Troops arrived at the top of the Arabian Gulf and made their way north, but in December 1915 the Turks surrounded them at Kut-al-Amara. Starvation forced a British surrender in April 1916. A renewed campaign in 1917 led to the fall of Baghdad in March. The British then continued north, taking Mosul in the autumn of 1918.

The Palestine campaign also ended in late 1918. In preparation for the final attack, the Arabs blew up parts of the Hejaz Railway, the Turks' supply line. Then on September 19, Allenby's

Among the troops under Allenby's command were members of the Imperial Camel Corps. These soldiers came from many countries, including Britain, Australia, New Zealand, India, and Egypt.

forces—British, French, Indians, and Anzacs—struck at places along the line, including Megiddo and El Afule. The Allies crushed the Turkish forces, and the Allies moved north, taking Damascus on October 1. On October 30, the Turks signed an armistice.

T.E. Lawrence and Emir Feisal had expected the Allies to reward their Arab supporters with independence once the Ottoman Empire was defeated. However, the British and French carved up its territory between them. In accordance with the British government's Balfour Declaration of 1917, Palestine later became a homeland for the Jews.

WAR IN AFRICA

In 1914, France and Britain both had large empires. They called on soldiers from their colonies in Africa and other places to fight for the Allied cause. The Germans also had some African colonies, and World War I battles took place on their territory. Togoland surrendered to the Allies in August 1914, Southwest Africa in May 1915, and the Cameroons in February 1916. However, German forces in East Africa continued fighting for four years, launching guerrilla raids over the Mozambique border even after the end of the war. They finally surrendered in November 1918.

Colonel T.E. Lawrence in Arab dress

Thomas Edward (T.E.) Lawrence was a brilliant scholar. He spoke fluent Arabic and had a thorough knowledge of Arab history. In 1926, he published *The Seven Pillars of Wisdom*, a history of the Arab revolt. In this excerpt he explains why he abandoned British army uniform for Arab dress.

The British army uniform is **khaki** (olive-brown) in color.

Feisal came from Mecca, the holiest city of Islam. It is now in Saudi Arabia.

Suddenly Feisal asked me if I would wear Arab clothes like his own while in camp. I should find it better for my own part, since it was a comfortable dress in which to live Arab-fashion as we must do. Besides, the tribesmen would then understand how to take me. The only wearers of **khaki** in their experience had been Turkish officers, before whom they took up an instinctive defense. If I wore **Meccan** clothes, they would behave to me as though I were really one of the leaders; and I might slip in and out of Feisal's tent without making a sensation which he had to explain away each time to strangers.

CHAPTER 6

1918

THE GERMAN OFFENSIVE

By 1918, the situation on the Western Front did not look good for the Allies. The Nivelle Offensive and Passchendaele (see pages 42–45) had been disasters. The Italians had been forced into retreat at Caporetto. Worse, about one million German reinforcements were moving in from the Eastern Front, which had closed down after Russia's withdrawal from the war. However, the Americans were also coming (see pages 40–41).

German commander Erich Ludendorff's plan to end the war using submarines had

failed, so he decided to risk an all-out land attack. Ludendorff believed that the large number of German troops made victory possible. To boost their chances, he introduced tactics that had worked in Russia. Among them was the use of storm troopers. Armed with light machine guns and flame-throwers, these soldiers acted independently and had a devastating effect.

The German offensive began in France on March 21, 1918. The aim was to hit the British hard at St. Quentin on the Somme,

separate them from the French, and drive them out to the coast. The preliminary attack was short, but very effective. Then the 750,000-strong German infantry surged forward. The war of movement returned as the Germans advanced 37 miles (60 km) in a week. The British, who numbered only 300,000, were forced to retreat. Paris was under threat.

The Germans kept up the offensive pressure for four months, but flaws in Ludendorff's plan slowly emerged. The speed of the advance and the war of attrition in 1916 and 1917 had exhausted the troops. Food supplies could not keep up with the men. Much of the artillery had been left behind, so German attacks grew lighter. Allied air attacks also began to weaken. Finally, there was no one to replace the thousands who had died in the fighting.

In April 1918, French general Ferdinand Foch was made commander in chief of all the Allied forces. The Americans made their first attack of the war at Cantigny in May. At Belleau Wood in June, they forced the Germans out of a long-held position. Foch saw that Allied strength was growing, while Germany was fading fast. In July, he decided that the time for counterattack had come.

THE WESTERN FRONT 1918

⊓⊓⊓	Hindenburg Line
——	Front line March 1918
◄—	German attacks
▓	German gains by July 1918
—►	Allied counter attacks
★	Major battle
░	Allied gains
– – –	Front line November 1918

North Sea
Ostend
Dunkirk
Ypres
N
BELGIUM
Mons
Arras
Somme River
PICARDY
Amiens
St Quentin
Cantigny
FRANCE
Belleau Wood
Rheims
Aisne River
ARGONNE
Meuse River
Verdun
LUX.
Châlons-sur-Marne
Paris
Marne River
CHAMPAGNE
St Mihiel

0   30 miles
0   50 km

THE FOURTEEN POINTS

By early 1918, American president Woodrow Wilson was already planning for peace. On January 8, he presented a program of Fourteen Points (right) to the U.S. Congress outlining his goals. This balanced list tried to be fair to all sides. Britain and France were wary of such idealism—they believed that Germany should be severely punished for its aggression. By the time the war was over, they had agreed that Wilson's Fourteen Points should provide the basis for the peace treaty discussions in Paris (see page 56).

Lt. Col. Frederick Wise was commander of the 2nd Battalion of the 5th U.S. Marines at Belleau Wood. His grisly account of the battle gives a sense of the tremendous losses that the Marines experienced at the Battle of Belleau Wood.

Program for the Peace of the World

By PRESIDENT WILSON January 8, 1918

I. Open covenants of peace, openly arrived at, after which there shall be no private international understandings of any kind, but diplomacy shall proceed always frankly and in the public view.

II. Absolute freedom of navigation upon the seas, outside territorial waters, alike in peace and in war, except as the seas may be closed in whole or in part by international action for the enforcement of international covenants.

III. The removal, so far as possible, of all economic barriers and the establishment of an equality of trade conditions among all the nations consenting to the peace and associating themselves for its maintenance.

IV. Adequate guarantees given and taken that national armaments will reduce to the lowest point consistent with domestic safety.

V. Free, open-minded, and absolutely impartial adjustment of all colonial claims, based upon a strict observance of the principle that in determining all such questions of sovereignty the interests of the population concerned must have equal weight with the equitable claims of the government whose title is to be determined.

VI. The evacuation of all Russian territory and such a settlement of all questions affecting Russia as will secure the best and freest coöperation of the other nations of the world in obtaining for her an unhampered and unembarrassed opportunity for the independent determination of her own political development and national policy, and assure her of a sincere welcome into the society of free nations under institutions of her own choosing; and, more than a welcome, assistance also of every kind that she may need and may herself desire. The treatment accorded Russia by her sister nations in the months to come will be the acid test of their goodwill, of their comprehension of her needs as distinguished from their own interests, and of their intelligent and unselfish sympathy.

VII. Belgium, the whole world will agree, must be evacuated and restored, without any attempt to limit the sovereignty which she enjoys in common with all other free nations. No other single act will serve as this will serve to restore confidence among the nations in the law which they have themselves set and determined for the government of their relations with one another. Without this healing act the whole structure and validity of international law is forever impaired.

VIII. All French territory should be freed and the invaded portions restored, and the wrong done to France by Prussia in 1871 in the matter of Alsace-Lorraine, which has unsettled the peace of the world for nearly fifty years, should be righted, in order that peace may once more be made secure in the interest of all.

IX. A readjustment of the frontiers of Italy should be effected along clearly recognizable lines of nationality.

X. The people of Austria-Hungary, whose place among the nations we wish to see safeguarded and assured, should be accorded the freest opportunity of autonomous development.

XI. Rumania, Serbia and Montenegro should be evacuated; occupied territories restored; Serbia accorded free and secure access to the sea; and the relations of the several Balkan States to one another determined by friendly counsel along historically established lines of allegiance and nationality; and international guarantees of the political and economic independence and territorial integrity of the several Balkan States should be entered into.

XII. The Turkish portions of the present Ottoman Empire should be assured a secure sovereignty, but the other nationalities which are now under Turkish rule should be assured an undoubted security of life and an absolutely unmolested opportunity of autonomous development, and the Dardanelles should be permanently opened as a free passage to the ships and commerce of all nations under international guarantees.

XIII. An independent Polish State should be erected which should include the territories inhabited by indisputably Polish populations, which should be assured a free and secure access to the sea, and whose political and economic independence and territorial integrity should be guaranteed by international covenant.

XIV. A general association of nations must be formed under specific covenants for the purpose of affording mutual guarantees of political independence and territorial integrity to great and small States alike.

Nothing in all our training had foreseen fighting like this. I passed nest after nest of German machine guns where Marines had fallen. Silhouetted in that ghastly light I could see splintered tree trunks and twisted limbs and the black mass of the forest stretching off. At the battle's end....I lined the men up. I had arrived May 31st with nine hundred and sixty-five men and twenty-six officers. Now before me stood three hundred and fifty men and six officers. Six hundred and fifteen men and nineteen officers were gone.

THE ALLIED COUNTER-OFFENSIVE

On July 15, 1918, the Germans launched their last attack of the war, a push toward Rheims and the Marne River. But the Allies held them back. Then, three days later, Foch struck back with a vengeance.

On July 18, the counter-offensive began with a joint operation by the French and Americans. With the aid of about five hundred tanks, they pushed the enemy line back about 6 miles (10 km). Next came a bigger push in which the British, Australians, and Canadians also played a major part. It began at 4:20 AM on August 8, near Amiens in Picardy. Again helped by tanks, the Allies overwhelmed the German defenses. By the evening they had taken over 110 sq. miles (285 sq. km) of land. Ludendorff called this the "black day" of the German army. There was no longer any real chance of

British Mark V tanks prepare to advance on the Hindenburg Line in September 1918. They carry devices called cribs which were lowered into wide trenches so that the tanks could roll across them.

Colonel George Patton

victory.

For most of August, the Allies continued to make gains in Picardy. Then, on September 12, the Americans attacked the St. Mihiel salient, south of Verdun (see map, page 50). Half a million U.S. troops took the salient in less than 24 hours. Among them was Colonel George Patton, who later played a major role in World War II. Soon after, Foch broadened the offensive to include the whole Western Front. On September 26, the final chapters of the war began to unfold.

The first stage of the new offensive was launched in the Champagne region, around the Meuse River and in nearby Argonne, a heavily wooded area. The Americans under General Pershing led the attack, with the French as backup. Early advances slowed as the Germans strengthened their defenses and rushed in reinforcements. However, by September the Americans were within reach of the Hindenburg Line. Meanwhile, the British under Haig had broken through the line farther north, a major accomplishment.

The Germans had nearly lost the war on the battlefield, and Ludendorff was cracking under the pressure. In late September,

This painting shows wounded, battle-weary British soldiers who have crossed the Hindenburg Line. In the background, the fighting continues.

he persuaded his government to ask the Allies for an armistice. The request was sent to President Woodrow Wilson on October 4. However, the peace terms that Wilson offered were harsh, and Ludendorff decided to continue the fight instead. Staring military defeat in the face, Germany also had serious problems at home (see pages 54–55).

THE AMERICAN HOME FRONT

Life in the U.S. was different after it entered the war, just as life on the European home fronts had changed earlier (see pages 28–29). The government-controlled War Industries Board oversaw production in all American factories and told them what to make. The War Labor Board regulated pay and working hours. Many women who already had jobs were switched over to war-related industries. The Committee on Public Information was set up to organize censorship and to explain the reasons for the war. It used film as a propaganda tool. One of its productions was *The Kaiser, the Beast of Berlin.*

***Im Westen Nichts Neues (All Quiet on the Western Front)* was written by Erich Maria Remarque,** a German who served in World War I. Since its publication in 1929, the novel has become a classic. It tells the story of a group of young German trench soldiers. Here the main character, Paul Bäumer, records his feelings in mid-1918.

Remarque is referring to the blue of the sky and gold of the sun.

This summer of 1918 is the bloodiest and the hardest. The days are like **angels in blue and gold**, rising up untouchable above the circle of destruction. Everyone knows that we are losing the war. Nobody talks about it much. We are retreating. We won't be able to attack again after this massive offensive. We have no more men and no more ammunition. But the campaign goes on—the dying continues... Summer 1918, never has life at the front been more bitter and more full of horror than when we are under fire, when the pallid faces are pressed into the mud and the fists are clenched and your whole being is saying, No! No! No, not now! Not now at the very last minute!

IM
WESTEN NICHTS NEUES

VON
ERICH MARIA REMARQUE

*

825.—850. TAUSEND

1 9 2 9
IM PROPYLÄEN-VERLAG / BERLIN

THE ARMISTICE

By 1918, food shortages in Germany were so severe that many people were forced to search through garbage to find something to eat.

By 1918, there was crisis on the German home front. Hunger and lack of faith in the war had led to growing discontent with imperial government. People's anger was made worse by the inequalities in German society. A flourishing black market allowed the rich to live well while everyone else existed on turnips and potatoes.

The Kaiser and his commanders had hoped that success in the March 1918 offensive (see page 50) would restore peaceful conditions. Its failure brought the opposite. People lost faith in their

leaders, and the demand for change grew. The Allies' reluctance to enter peace negotiations with the imperial regime added to the pressure for reform.

Finally, on September 30, Kaiser Wilhelm II signed a decree that brought democratic parliamentary government to Germany. Prince Max von Baden was made the new chancellor (chief minister). It became his duty, rather than the army's, to negotiate an armistice with the Allies. This was exactly what army commander Erich Ludendorff wanted. The responsibility for Germany's military failure was his. However, he began to blame civilians, claiming that they had not supported the army enough. The decision to ask the Allies for an armistice was also his—but the request was made by the chancellor. By then rejecting President Wilson's peace terms, Ludendorff was able to insist that the army had always wished to continue fighting (see page 59).

The Kaiser defeated Ludendorff on October 26, but as peace terms still could not be reached, the fighting continued. Then the German authorities ordered the fleet to begin a new campaign at sea. German sailors had been in port since 1916 (see

German officials (standing) arrive to sign the armistice at 5:00 on the morning of November 11, 1918. This momentous event took place in a railway car in the Forest of Compiègne, northern France.

pages 26-27). During that time, their resentment of tyrannical officers and of the government had grown. On October 29, the sailors mutinied in Kiel and Wilhelmshaven.

Soon the whole country was in an uproar and demanded the Kaiser's removal from office. On November 8, he fled from Berlin, and the next day he abdicated his power. Germany became a republic, led by Friedrich Ebert, and two days later the armistice was signed. At 11 A.M. on November, 11, after more than four years of bloody battle, the cease-fire began.

THE BATTLE OF VITTORIO VENETO

The fighting on the Western Front ended with the November 11 cease-fire. On the Salonika Front (see page 23), the Bulgarians had already signed an armistice on September 29. In the Middle East, the Turks had signed an armistice on October 30 (see page 49). Italy's defeat at Caporetto (see page 45) was finally reversed on November 4, when the Austrian army was defeated by a joint Allied force at Vittorio Veneto. It was all over.

Vera Brittain served as a VAD nurse (see page 30) during the war, in London, Malta, and France. In 1933, she published an autobiography called *Testament of Youth*, which describes her experiences. Both her brother Edward, and the man she had hoped to marry, Roland, died in the fighting. When the cease-fire began, Vera Brittain was in London. Here she tells of the emotions that she experienced at that time.

When the sound of victorious guns burst over London at 11 a.m. on November 11th 1918, the men and women who looked incredulously into each other's faces did not cry jubilantly: "We've won the War!" They only said: "The War is over."... Late that evening, when supper was over, a group of elated V.A.D.s who were anxious to walk through Westminster and Whitehall to Buckingham Palace prevailed upon me to join them... I detached myself from the others and walked slowly up Whitehall, with my heart sinking in a sudden cold dismay... For the first time I realized, with all that full realization meant, how completely everything that had hitherto made up my life had vanished with Edward and Roland... The War was over; a new age was beginning; but the dead were dead and would never return.

Desagneaux is referring to the lights of German flares and rockets, not real fireworks.

Henri Desagneaux (see page 13) was still in the trenches when the armistice was signed. This is how he recorded the event.

11 November

Firework display continued all night over in the enemy camp. At 6 a.m., we hear on the radio that the armistice has been signed. The end of hostilities is fixed for 11 a.m. At 11 a.m. it's all over, we are no longer at war. What joy—the champagne flows, the attack won't take place. There's a smile on everyone's lips, no more fighting, we'll be able to move without fearing a bullet, a shell, a rocket, or gas—the war is over!

THE AFTERMATH

The aftermath of World War I had two sides: political and personal. The main political questions were resolved—at least temporarily—in the Treaty of Versailles, which was drawn up just outside Paris in 1919. Personal aspects, from the traumas of shell shock (see box, page 57), injuries, to family bereavement over the deaths of soldiers in combat, as well as adjustments in daily life, were addressed in many different ways, with different degrees of success.

The conference that intended to work out a peace settlement began in Paris, France, on January 18, 1919. Members of twenty-seven nations attended, but the leading Allied participants were the American and French presidents, Woodrow Wilson and Georges Clemenceau, and the British prime minister, David Lloyd George. Italian prime minister Vittorio Orlando was another important contributor. The Germans sat on the sidelines waiting to hear their fate. Wilson's Fourteen Points, the starting point for the talks, outlined a plan based on democracy, no loss of land or reparations, and the formation of a League of Nations to work together for peace.

Much wrangling followed, especially between the idealistic Wilson and the more practical—and vengeful—Clemenceau. The Treaty of Versailles was signed on June 28, 1919. Some of the Fourteen Points were included, such as the League of Nations. However, the treatment of Germany was far more severe than Wilson had envisioned. Germany was declared responsible for the war, and was forced to pay huge reparations for the damage caused by the conflict. In addition, the size of its armed forces was strictly limited, and much of its territories were taken away.

The Germans had no choice but to meet the treaty's demands. However, the great bitterness and economic upheaval caused by the Versailles agreement directly contributed to the rise of Adolf Hitler and the outbreak of World War II only twenty years later, in 1939.

Ironically, the Treaty of Versailles was never approved by the U.S. Congress, whose leaders disagreed with the treaty's terms. A separate peace was later negotiated between the United States and Germany. However, President Wilson was awarded the 1919 Nobel Peace Prize for his efforts, and he earned worldwide admiration as a man of reconciliation.

This famous painting by Sir William Orpen shows the signing of the Treaty of Versailles in 1919.

Wilfred Owen served with the Artists' Rifles and Manchester Regiment. His poems were first published in 1920, two years after his death.

PAYING THE PRICE

About nine million men died in the World War I. Many of those who survived had lost limbs or suffered other serious wounds. About 12 percent of the wounded had facial injuries. It was especially difficult for some of these men to become part of everyday civilian life once again. Thousands of soldiers also suffered from psychological disorders brought on by what they had witnessed. "Shell shock" took many forms. Some men could not stop shaking, while others were literally paralyzed. Some laughed hysterically or became delusional or were haunted by nightmares.

English war poet Wilfred Owen (above) became shell-shocked in spring 1917. He went to Craiglockhart Hospital in Scotland for treatment, then returned to France, where he was killed a week before the armistice. This is part of his poem "Disabled."

He sat in a wheeled chair, waiting for dark,
And shivered in his ghastly suit of grey,
Legless, sewn short at elbow. Through the park
Voices of boys rang saddening like a hymn,
Voices of play and pleasure after day,
Till gathering sleep had mothered them from him.
…
Now, he will spend a few sick years in institutes,
And do what things the rules consider wise,
And take whatever pity they may dole.
To-night he noticed how the women's eyes
Passed from him to the strong men that were
    whole.
How cold and late it is! Why don't they come
And put him into bed? Why don't they come?

This article of the Treaty of Versailles made Germany responsible for the war and demanded reparations.

ARTICLE 231. The Allied and Associated Governments affirm and Germany accepts the responsibility of Germany and her allies for causing all the loss and damage to which the Allied and Associated Governments and their nationals have been subjected as a consequence of the war imposed upon them by the aggression of Germany and her allies…

The Treaty of Versailles, showing the signatures and wax seals of some participants

CONCLUSION

The world that emerged from the cataclysm of World War I was very different from the one that had entered it more than four years earlier. A generation of young men—about 5.4 million from the Allies and about 3.6 million from the Central Powers—had been killed. The civilian population was plunged into mourning. Four empires had fallen, and the map of the world had been redrawn. The United States had taken on a new role as a true international power. The effects were so profound and lasting that the conflict became known as the Great War.

Redefining the world's boundaries, as outlined at Versailles, was a complicated matter. Alsace-Lorraine was returned to France. A corner of northeast Germany became part of Poland, which was now free from Russian rule, as were the Baltic states of Estonia, Latvia, and Lithuania. The Rhineland area between France and Germany was occupied by the Allies and the Saarland handed over to League of Nations control for a period of fifteen years. Austria, Hungary, Czechoslovakia, and Yugoslavia were carved out of the old Austro-Hungarian Empire.

Farther afield, France and Britain divided the former German colonies in Africa and the former Turkish territories in the Middle East between themselves. Most of Turkey was given to Greece, but the Turks seized it back and proclaimed an independent republic in 1923.

In this photograph, taken in 1933, Field Marshal Paul von Hindenburg, by then German president, and Adolf Hitler, the new chancellor, sit side by side.

THE NEW EUROPE

Lost by Russia

Lost by Germany

Former Austro-Hungarian Empire

Rhineland area (occupied by Allies)

League of Nations control

0 — 400 miles
0 — 600 km

GREAT BRITAIN · North Sea · DENMARK · Baltic Sea · ESTONIA · LATVIA · LITHUANIA · Danzig · NETH. · GERMANY · POLAND · BELGIUM · Saarland · LUX. · Alsace-Lorraine · CZECHOSLOVAKIA · FRANCE · SWITZ. · AUSTRIA · HUNGARY · ROMANIA · RUSSIA · YUGOSLAVIA · ITALY · BULGARIA · Black Sea · Mediterranean Sea · N

The legacy of all this change was a time of instability. As before the war, people of one nationality—the Germans in Poland, for example—found themselves ruled by another country. The League of Nations was unable to prevent growing tension. The Germans began to reassert themselves and, in 1933, Nazi leader Adolf Hitler came to power.

Hitler used the "stab in the back" theory—Ludendorff's claim that the army had been betrayed by civilians (see page 54)—to justify attacks on anyone who did not agree with his political views. He also assured the Germans, humiliated by the Treaty of Versailles, that their nation would soon be great again. Another world war was in the making.

"For the Fallen," a poem by Laurence Binyon, who served with the Red Cross during the war, is often read on the anniversary of Armistice Day, November 11. This verse comes from that poem.

They shall grow not old, as we that are left grow old:
Age shall not weary them, nor the years condemn.
At the going down of the sun and in the morning
We will remember them.

Many who experienced the horror of trench warfare later described their experiences in words and pictures. Otto Dix was a German artist who fought in the trenches. In words such as these, as well as in his paintings, he conjured up the nightmare of the suffering he experienced.

Lice, rats, barbed wire, fleas, shells, bombs, underground caves, corpses, blood, liquor, mice, cats, artillery, filth, bullets, mortars, fire, steel: that is what war is. It is the work of the devil.

REMEMBERING THE FALLEN

After the war, memorials to the dead were built on the battlefields and in the hometowns and villages of those who died. They are to this day places of pilgrimage. Those who sacrificed their lives are remembered particularly on Armistice Day, November 11, when many official ceremonies are held at the memorials and other places. The red poppies that covered the battlefields of Flanders in the summer have become a symbol of the dead and in Britain are worn as a tribute.

The opening ceremony, in 1936, of the memorial to the soldiers who died at Vimy Ridge in France

GLOSSARY

Allies The countries that formed the Triple Entente in 1907 (Britain, France, and Russia) and later opposed the Central Powers in World War I. The term also applies to all the other countries that joined their side, including Belgium and Japan (from 1914), Italy (1915) and the United States (1917).

Anzac A member of the Australian and New Zealand Army Corps.

armistice An official agreement between opposing sides in a war to stop fighting.

arms race Rivalry between countries rushing to arm themselves with the best and most modern weapons, tanks, other military equipment.

artillery The collective name for cannons and other heavy guns with barrels of a caliber (diameter) of over 20 mm.

attrition The gradual process of wearing something or someone down in order to overcome them.

Balfour Declaration A letter written by British foreign secretary Arthur Balfour in November 1917. It said that the British government approved the establishment of a Jewish homeland in Palestine. The homeland became known as Israel in 1948.

Balkans A peninsula in southeastern Europe that in World War I contained the countries of Albania, Bulgaria, Greece, Montenegro, Romania, Serbia, and the European part of the Ottoman Empire.

bayonet A long, thin blade that is attached to a gun so that it extends beyond the end of the barrel. Bayonets are used in hand-to-hand combat.

black market Illegal trade in goods that have been officially restricted by government rationing.

blockade The blocking of access to a particular area in order to prevent people or supplies from getting in.

Bolshevik A member of the group of Communists that seized power in Russia in 1917. The word "Bolshevik" means "majority," because the Bolsheviks formed the larger part of the Russian Social Democratic Party.

British Expeditionary Force (BEF) The first troops that left Britain for mainland Europe in 1914. They were all professional soldiers under the command of Sir John French.

cavalry Troops on horseback.

Central Powers The countries that fought against the Allies in World War I. They were Germany and Austria-Hungary, both members of the Triple Alliance from 1882, the Ottoman Empire (from 1914), and Bulgaria (1915).

conscientious objector A person who refuses to fight in a war for reasons of conscience —because of the belief that physical violence is morally wrong.

conscription Compulsory (mandatory) service in the armed forces.

convoy A group of merchant ships escorted by a group of battleships for its protection.

corps A group of soldiers, made up of at least two divisions.

counter-battery A battle technique in which artillery from opposing sides fire on each other rather than on attacking troops.

court-martial To try someone in a military court of law.

division A group of soldiers large enough to act independently. In World War I, French divisions usually had between ten and twelve thousand soldiers. British divisions had about fifteen thousand soldiers.

Eastern Front The areas of Eastern Europe where opposing armies fought each other during World War I.

Entente Cordiale The alliance formed between Britain and France in 1904. The name is French for "friendly understanding."

field telephone A special type of telephone that can be used in an area where battle is taking place.

flamethrower A weapon that shoots out a stream of burning gas or paraffin (a flammable wax).

Flanders An area of Europe that includes parts of Belgium, northern France, and the Netherlands.

front line The area of a battlefield reached by the most advanced troops of opposing armies, where they face and fight each another directly.

General Staff The group of officers that help military commanders plan and carry out their operations.

guerrilla A member of a small, often unofficial fighting force.

Guerrillas generally specialize in surprise attacks and sabotage.

Hindenburg Line A long line of trenches and other fortifications on the Western Front, to which the Germans withdrew in 1917.

home front The parts of countries involved in the war where no fighting took place, but where civilians contributed to the war effort by making weapons or growing food, for example.

howitzer A type of cannon that fired shells high into the air.

incendiary bullet A bullet that is specially designed to start a fire once it hits a target.

infantry Soldiers who fight on foot.

isolationism A policy to not participate in international politics.

minesweeper A navy ship that detects mines, then clears or neutralizes them so that they cannot explode.

mobilize To assemble troops and prepare for action.

munitions Ammunition, arms, and other military equipment.

mustard gas A yellow gas used as a chemical weapon. It caused blisters, burns to the skin and lungs, and sometimes blindness.

No Man's Land The unoccupied area between the front-line trenches of opposing armies.

offensive A major military attack that involves many groups of soldiers acting together to achieve a particular goal.

Ottoman Empire The former empire of the Ottoman Turks, sometimes also known as the Turkish Empire. It lasted from the late twelfth century to the end of World War I. At its height it covered a vast area including parts of Russia, the Middle East, North Africa, and southern Europe, as well as Turkey itself.

outflanking A military maneuver that involves going around the flank (side) of the enemy, then turning back to surround them.

phosgene A poisonous, colorless gas used as a chemical weapon. It caused victims to choke to death slowly.

propaganda Biased information designed to support a particular cause or damage the reputation of an enemy.

rationing Limiting the availability of food, and sometimes other goods, to small, fixed amounts.

reconnaissance The act of gathering information about enemy activities by flying over their trenches, for example.

reparations Compensation for damage caused in a war. The Germans were ordered to pay reparations after the war in the form of ships, raw materials and other goods, as well as money.

salient A front-line bulge that extends into enemy territory.

Serbs A Slavic people whose language is Serbo-Croat. Before World War I, some Serbs lived in the kingdom of Serbia, others in the Austro-Hungarian Empire.

shell Any of various types of explosive missile fired by artillery. Some shells explode in the air, others explode when they hit a target.

shrapnel Shells containing bullets and pieces of metal that are scattered all around when the shells explode. The word also refers to the bullets and metal pieces themselves.

Slavs A group of peoples from Eastern Europe and Northwest Asia who speak Slavic languages such as Russian, Polish, and Serbo-Croat.

storm trooper A German soldier who did not advance on enemy lines with the main body of troops, but acted independently. Storm troopers used light but deadly weapons such as machine guns and flame throwers.

torpedo A cigar-shaped missile that propels itself along under water and is used to attack ships and submarines.

trench fever An infectious disease that causes fever and pain in joints, bones, and muscles. It is transmitted by bites from body lice.

trench foot A type of frostbite caused by standing in cold water for a long time. It made feet swell, then go numb. When the swelling went down, the pain became intense.

Triple Alliance The alliance formed by Austria-Hungary, Germany, and Italy in 1882.

Triple Entente The alliance formed by Britain, France, and Russia in 1907.

U-boat A German submarine. The term is short for *Unterseeboot*, German for "undersea boat."

Western Front The areas of France and Belgium in Western Europe where opposing armies faced each other in combat during World War I.

INDEX